BURSTING
at the
SEAMS

Human Growth and the Future of Clothes

ANNIKA THOMAS

Website: metamorfos.se

Publisher: BoD · Books on Demand, Östermalmstorg 1,
114 42 Stockholm, bod@bod.se
Print: Libri Plureos GmbH, Friedensallee 273,
22763 Hamburg, Tyskland
ISBN: 978-91-8057-543-0

*To the women and men who are focused on
reinventing clothes, the clothing industry
and the system behind it.*

Table of Contents

PROLOGUE   A Holistic Mindset   1

Tracing a Hidden Thread   7

INTRODUCTION   A Meta Morphosis   16

Integrating Perspectives   19

PART I – COMMON THREADS   21

THE WORN-OUT STORY   In the Midst of a Shift   23

Hacking Fashion   27

A System of Waste   30

Outdated Mindsets   34

Redirecting Growth   41

Asking the Right Questions   43

WHERE DID WE COME FROM?   The Cultural Backdrop   45

Hidden Stories   47

A Very Different Culture   51

The Mother Goddess   54

Destructive Forces   59

The Minoan Culture   62

The Demise of the Goddess   65

CULTURE AS A SHAPING MOLD   Image Versus Word   68

Two Sides of a Whole   72

From Wholeness to Separation   77

Ideals of Beauty   79

PART II– DRESSED FOR GROWTH   85

The Essence of Clothing Design   86

A Closer Look at Identity   89

The Wisdom of the Pyramid 100

Natural Human Growth 104

A SET OF NEEDS Basic Needs 108

A Need to Belong 111

Esteem Needs 114

Aesthetic Needs 117

Inner Balance 119

Integration 125

Unity 128

PART III – THE ART OF DESIGNING IDENTITY 131

The Wardrobe Speaks 132

A Language of the Psyche 135

Our Energy Field 137

COLORS A Language of Light 140

Color Hues 144

Color Brightness 145

Color Saturation 147

Three Faces of Color 148

Color Graphics 150

Color Interpretation 152

Red 154

Orange 155

Yellow 156

Green 157

Turquoise 158

Blue 159

Purple 161

	Using Colors as Tools	163
SHAPES	Dynamic Blueprints	164
	A Point of Focus	169
	The Circle of Wholeness	169
	The Dividing Line	171
	Triangle Dynamics	172
	The Stable Square	173
	Expansion of Consciousness	174
	Pentagram	175
	Hexagram	176
	Heptagram	177
PATTERNS	Impact on Repeat	178
	Basic Life Patterns	183
	Our Inner Climate	190
	Fractal Patterns	192
CLOTHING STYLES	Dressing Archetypes	194
	Tweaking our Clothing Style	199
	Using Clothes as Tools	202

PART IV – TOWARDS A NEW STORY — 207

	A New Paradigm	208
	Visionary Art & Design	210
	Taking Beauty Seriously	213
	And the New Story Begins	216
EPILOGUE	The Fabric of Life	221

| List of References | 223 |
| About the Author | 225 |

A Holistic Mindset

I am a holistic designer. Even though a holistic perspective – where we look at the interconnection between the parts of something to understand it more fully – is known to many, my statement is often followed by a raised eyebrow. To eyes that begin to wander. What does it mean when holistic and design are combined? The confusion might be due to my own inability to explain, in a short and clear way, what holistic means in relation to clothes. When I try, I falter. Apparently more space is needed to explore and explain what it really means, maybe even to myself. Writing a book often has this magical component – it takes you through a process where things that might have been a bit muddled become more clear.

With *Bursting at the Seams* I invite you to join me on the thought provoking journey this book turned out to be, as I thoroughly explored the wide-ranging and interrelated parts that are connected to clothes.

So can a holistic view of our everyday clothes really shed light upon how we relate to them as well as our approach to design and ways of manufacturing? Is it possible to reach a deeper understanding, along with ideas for new ways to deal with present challenges, through considering how its different parts are tied together?

One example that clearly demonstrates the difference between our common approach to things and one that is holistic is Western medicine. Even though there are amazing inventions and progress in this field, it is still shaped by our present narrative and the mindsets born out of it. A person with a physical problem is usually looked at from a mechanistic perspective, where the body is regarded as an assembly of separate parts. A medication is prescribed to deal with the symptoms from the part in focus. This tends to shut down the important alarm system of the body, while the complex interconnections between things like lifestyle, social connections, emotional and mental struggles are ignored.

A holistic approach, on the other hand, would interpret symptoms and pain as if the body is saying, or sometimes even screaming: "Hey… pay attention! Something is going on in this intricately interrelated system that you need to take a closer look at to understand!" This does not mean that symptoms should be ignored, or that there are no benefits from medication, but that the deeper root causes of a condition have to be addressed to find permanent healing.

So is there a similar fragmented mindset in the field of clothes? We all know that there are serious issues regarding beauty and appearance ideals, consumption patterns as well as clothing manufacturing with devastating social, economic and ecological effects. To try to counteract some of the negative consequences the clothing industry tends to focus on natural materials, recycling and the chemicals used to produce our garments. While this is necessary and important, it is still like tending to one symptom. If we instead look at all issues regarding clothes as parts of a larger problem, it might shed new light upon the deeper causes and help us find a probable common source.

What is absolutely certain is that clothes cannot be taken out of a larger context. To make sense of the various reasons why we choose to wear certain kinds of clothes we have to take a closer look at cultural ideals as well as the development of our identity.

Apart from their aesthetic side clothes are designed to fill different needs for the person wearing them. Some of these are purely practical, while others relate to psychological needs, closely tied to how we see ourselves. There are also deeper needs. So how would clothes change if our need for inner development was as important as our need for protection against things like cold temperatures? What would happen to the garments we wear if beauty ideals became obsolete? One thing is certain: As we evolve new needs emerge. Unless we figure out what those are, and find ways to develop clothes to also fill these needs, we will outgrow them. Their seams will begin to burst.

Since clothes, along with manmade systems and entire industries, are also intricately connected to culture and the prevailing paradigm, it seems necessary to take a deeper look into our past to trace the probable origins of the mindsets and belief systems that have shaped Western civilization. Thus even more puzzle pieces are added to our holistic design field, pieces that are usually related to the more hidden, inner realms of human experience. Some of these are the rise of culture and the evolution of language along with their somewhat obscure causes and interconnections. Their effect on the human psyche is another. All these relevant factors can help us discern a common pattern and an overall perspective.

> The real voyage of discovery
> consists not in seeking out new landscapes
> but in having new eyes.
> *Marcel Proust*

We cannot fully understand things holistically unless we *look from* a place that is more whole. Bear with me as I try to explain what I mean by that.

We live in a time where there is an abundance of knowledge and to state what we see as Truth we usually refer to science. The problem here is that when we believe we know something we tend to stop there, no longer open to other possibilities or different ways of understanding things. Instead of pushing the limits of what we understand regarding life and the nature of things – which is the *true* essence of science – this keeps us stuck within certain limits.

As parts of a culture that tends to rely primarily on the rational mind at the expense of intuition or inner experiences, we are groomed for imbalance. This kind of cultural climate can never be sustainable. With this skewed perception we are set on a journey as with an unbalanced rudder, that constantly steers off course, which will take us far from where we want to go. Despite progress in some areas we would continue to be an unsustainable society with polarization, conflict and gender imbalances, while our natural habitats slowly disappear.

When one part is overvalued – in the human psyche as well as our collective consciousness – its polar opposite is pushed aside. It becomes a shadow field that is looked down upon. This blindspot has something important to tell us about personal and cultural unfoldment.

This imbalance is the reason why some things we will explore in this book might challenge the way we are used to look at life, civilization and the human identity. Even though there has been a gradual acceptance over the last decades of some alternative fields that are more connected to inner, deeper realities such as yoga, meditation and breath-work, some biases remain. This might be the reason why homeopathy, acupuncture, energy medicine, healing and astrology, (to name a few) are still trivialized and labeled "woo woo" by many.

Groundbreaking research, following rigorous scientific methods, has been conducted in some of these fields and clearly show their validity, but since they are still not accepted by large parts of the scientific community they remain unacknowledged. The issue is thus *not* about what can be scientifically proven, but rather points to a resistance to accept the existence, and value, of deeper realities.

Even though love, intuition, the existence of a soul, or how we are affected by the colors and patterns of the clothes we wear is difficult to weigh, measure or explain logically, this does not mean it is not real. If I have a deep connection to what I experience as my soul and someone tells me there is no scientific proof for a soul, these are just two different perspectives. One that trusts the rational mind and one that relies on inner experiences. From a holistic perspective we can see how these are simply two sides of a whole. Both parts are present within each of us and none is better, or more true, than the other. What is important is to find a healthy interaction and balance between them.

There are many things in our complex world that cannot be measured or proven. Luckily there are other ways of knowing. Some things must be seen through experiences that only make sense over time, while others are highlighted by intuitive insights. Wisdom emerges from a state of not-knowing and the lucid awareness of our heart – this higher faculty we all have access to – always remains the best wayshower.

Truth is, after all, a moving target. It evolves and morphs, and is always the result of challenging the established limits of thought to some degree. We need to be humble to the fact that what we believe always changes. As we face the challenges of our time, along with the risk of extinction on the one hand and the possibility to create a more conscious, sustainable and thriving society on the other, our best option is respect for different kinds of knowing and an openness to a variety of ways to look at the world. To see things differently does not have to be a conflict. Whether it regards the human psyche, the clothes we wear, manmade systems or civilizations, different perspectives help us recognize inner drivers as well as the dynamics of different phenomena.

The ability to remain in a state of not-knowing, with an open mind and heart, is a superpower that allows us to curiously explore possibilities. Learning to relate to complexity, without overvaluing one side of things while dismissing another, is part of our human evolution.

> The ability to observe without evaluating
> is the highest form of intelligence.
> *Krishnamurti*

In a creative pursuit, and when we are trying to find solutions to specific problems, our minds need to work laterally and involve the unique approach of both sides of our brains. Our right-brain, with its ability to freely imagine things and grasp complex interconnections, has to be invited on to the arena even though its ways of knowing are not rational, nor easily provable. As in any creative process we need to approach new ideas with an open mind and a willingness to learn, rather than falling into the trap of judging and dismissing things.

I have approached my subject – human growth and the future of clothes – with this kind of open mindset, without any need to hastily label things as true or false, nor dismissing any piece of information that first seemed questionable. I stored these at the back of my mind as "intriguing possibilities". A few of them eventually made sense in the larger picture.

So welcome to join me on this explorative journey! We will travel through meandering paths where ancient wisdom, intuition and inner experiences are interwoven with scientific knowledge, analysis and categorizations. On this trail, where inner and outer realities merge, limiting beliefs will be questioned and interesting connections scrutinized.

Even though I believe that the conclusions in this book make sense, I have no need, nor intention, to claim them as the Right way forward. I continue to ask the question "What if…?" instead of presenting any cemented truth. This book thus remains a journey of exploration meant to challenge the status quo, widen our perspectives and point to possible new paths. My best hope is that this can bring inspiration and lead to innovative ideas for future clothes.

Tracing a Hidden Thread

As I left our San Francisco head office I felt anxious. Even scared. I knew, in the depth of my heart, that I did not belong to the world of fashion and that I needed to do something about it. Up until a year before I had believed that I did. But then, on my summer holidays, I had met a new friend who talked to me about an impending paradigm shift, the need to find our deeper calling and a different kind of spirituality beyond religion. He even talked about God in a way that was new to me. Since I had been brought up more or less without any organized religion, and saw myself as a skeptical agnostic, I felt a bit uneasy. But as this man talked there was this profound sense of already knowing the things he talked about, and an immediate feeling of coming home to a deeper part of myself. It shook me to my core and was as wonderful as deeply confusing. What was happening to me? And who was I really?

Returning home to everyday life was difficult. The gut feeling that I needed to find a deeper purpose to what I was already doing was so strong that the things that had used to fill my days didn't feel meaningful anymore. I had so many questions and the only thing that truly inspired me was to explore the deeper aspects of life. Zooming out to grasp a larger perspective. As I did, a new conviction grew: We cannot design clothes that are good for us unless we truly understand the person wearing them. Another way of working with clothes, built on a different set of values than those of modern culture, as well as awareness of the development of identity, was possible. Clothes that were actually beneficial to the person who wore them. I had no idea what this meant, or how they would look, but my determination to find out grew by each day. I knew I would get there if I just trusted what my heart told me.

Still, there were days when I questioned if I was delusional and if what had happened to me had made me lose it. Some people around me seemed to think so. My friends and colleagues didn't understand what I was going through, even though I only shared a small part of it. I felt very lonely. At the same time I was happier than I had ever been, since I felt connected to a part of myself that felt real and true. My life had taken on a deeper meaning.

As head of design for the Scandinavian branch of a multinational clothing company I earned a lot of money. I also led what many would consider a very glamorous life; traveling around the world, meeting famous artists and rock stars. But that didn't make me happy since there was no room for me to grow. My job was to focus on what our costumers would want the next season. Looking further into the future was not an option.

For a time I tried to implement some positive changes, like raising the quality of our garments and scrutinizing the values behind our work. But instead of contributing to something positive, I became acutely aware of the dark side of fashion. I saw how models, groomed to some unreal perfection, increased the insecurities of normal people. I noticed the mechanics behind how costumers were seduced and exploited, through flashy and extremely expensive commercials, to believe that their lives would actually be better if they wore our clothes. How hunger for profit had become more important than quality and ethics. I was appalled. Why hadn't I seen this before? Could I really continue to be a part of this madness?

Every day that went by made it more impossible to stay. I remember telling a friend that I felt like an eagle with my wings clipped at work. I knew that leaving would be a point of no return that would ruin the career I had put so much energy and effort into. But what else could I do? My biggest problem was how to support myself. Since my heart was no longer in it, it would even be difficult for me to take on freelance jobs. But my inner guidance was relentless and increasingly loud. I simply had to take my own questions and hunches seriously.

As my courage and determination grew, a bold decision finally gained enough momentum. One day I knocked on my boss' door and told him I had decided to quit. He seemed shocked and unable to believe that I would simply leave at the top of my career. A few months later, as I closed the door to my office for the last time, I really did leave the world of fashion. This was in the mid 1980's and I felt certain that a paradigm shift would occur within a decade, maybe two. I was as impatient as naive, but truly curious and excited about the path I saw ahead for myself: a quest to find a deeper and more meaningful way to work with clothes. I knew I would have to dig deep. Convinced that I was doing what I was called to do, I felt sure that the rest of my life, like having an income and a place to live, would get sorted. Luckily I had some money put aside which would keep me afloat for a while.

> Two roads diverged in a wood and I -
> I took the one less traveled by,
> and that has made all the difference.
> *Robert Frost*

My journey turned out to be far from a pleasant ride, though. I realized that my first step had to be to thoroughly explore my own identity to begin to grasp the connection to the clothes I wore. I was ruthless in search of my core being. Within a year I had left, lost or gotten rid of practically everything that I had identified with: my marriage, my home, most of my belongings, old friends and, of course, my job. Since eating gave me comfort in a time that was quite scary, I had also gained more than 30 pounds, so my slim and fit body was also gone. My personal life hardly existed anymore and I retreated into a kind of isolation. In hindsight I can understand what a perfect setup this was to speed up my inner development. But it was as confusing as deeply painful.

In order to find out why clothes had become such an important part of my life, I took a serious look at my childhood and adolescence. I realized that I had been very confused about how, and who, to be. Growing up with a single mum required quite a lot of self-sufficiency. She had enough to cope with, so I couldn't give her any extra trouble. There was also a lot of focus on masculine qualities. Even if these were invaluable lessons that have helped me throughout my life, the numerable times I had to cope on my own, in situations I was really too young to handle, left me feeling very insecure.

In many ways it was a harsh environment for a sensitive and quite introvert child like me, who was deeply connected to my inner life and leaned towards many feminine characteristics. I didn't feel seen or understood. As a consequence I couldn't see and appreciate my own qualities. As time went by the door to my true Self slowly closed – a disconnection that led to a lack of self-worth. I felt lost and insecure, but anxiously hiding it. Inadequate, trying to live up to expectations. Single mothers were unusual in Sweden at the time (I didn't know of anyone else in our area) and mum told me and my sister to not tell anyone about our family situation. We were to pretend to the outer world that we were just like everybody else, which further enforced the necessity to create a fake, controlled front.

Looking back, it seemed clear to me why such a deep split had formed between my inner Self and the part I presented to the world, and why my core identity had been shoved into oblivion. No wonder it had led to an exaggerated identification with my outer persona. Since I was also a lover of beauty, I began making my own clothes at an early age. They gave me a silent promise to provide the confidence and the qualities I lacked. Like some kind of magic.

Eventually I lost myself in cultural ideals and became more or less addicted to fashion, telling me, through the language of clothes, which attitudes and values were "the right" ones. Telling me how to be. At the time it felt fun though, and it was exciting to try to be on the leading edge of changing cultural ideals. I felt seen. And good enough. Which, in hindsight, was such an obvious compensation.

When it was time to choose a career I was hesitant. Eventually I went for design college, even though I knew I didn't fit the mold of a typical designer. I couldn't quite put my finger on what was different about me, though. Immediately after my graduation I was hired by a clothing company and the mix of employers that followed gave me the perfect combination of skill and experience in all the different aspects of the clothing business, ranging from sales to production, as well as design and the construction of garment patterns. This, in combination with an ability to intuit collective trends and translate these to clothing styles, helped me advance.

Focused as I was on my work and everyday life, I barely noticed when a larger part of me began to make itself known. The first signs were a puzzling anger. As a designer of clothes others would approach me with the question: "What should I wear this season?" I had begun to feel this immediate explosion of anger as they asked. I tried to hide it and answer in a nice way, but it was confusing. After giving it some thought I realized it had to do with the stupidity of conforming to the unspoken rules of fashion. But that didn't explain my explosive reaction. Why did this seem so important to me? Below the surface of my awareness, the seams of my fashionable 2nd skin were beginning to burst.

And now, a few years later, this outer skin of mine had completely burst open, leaving me raw and vulnerable. It was like I had spun a chrysalis around myself while the person I had been was dissolving inside of it. Understanding who I was behind my persona seemed crucial. I saw an astrologer who helped me explore my personal horoscope. Since it revealed deeply hidden traits, inner conflicts as well as innate gifts and talents, it was a real eyeopener. I felt truly seen for the first time in my life. It also showed me how I needed to grow. When I realized that the different planets, signs, houses, elements and aspects of astrology could be seen as a non-verbal language of energy, it triggered a strong feeling that I was on to something important that could help me solve the riddle of how to design clothes in a different way.

To explore this further I began to study astrological psychology, which was like learning a new and much deeper language, based on symbols, energetic processes and elemental forces. Excited I realized that if I could figure out how these energetic patterns were connected to colors, visual patterns and clothing styles, it could be used to influence our psyche in the process of balancing and integrating different parts. It would give us tools to transform and expand identity.

Psychoanalysis helped me find clarity about how I had been limited by my conditioning. I embarked on a journey of art therapy, began to meditate and practice yoga. I also attended a myriad of courses, workshops and retreats, and practiced many different methods of shadow work, self growth and healing, all while reading tons of books on psycho-spiritual processes, healing, esoteric teachings, evolution theories and everything I could find about the deeper aspects of colors and shapes, archetypes, symbols and dreams.

But instead of breaking through to a sense of inner peace, I slowly reached rock bottom. I remember having this overwhelming sense of being stuck in a crack between two worlds. I had left one but didn't know how to reach the other. It felt *totally* impossible to bridge the gap between the deeper knowledge I had found and my work as a designer. While my inner Self filled my being with clarity and insights, my personal self was frail, insecure and ungrounded. The only clothes I felt like wearing were shapeless garments in black or white. It was extremely painful and at one point I even made plans to end my life. What saved me was a deep inner knowing that I was going through some necessary metamorphosis and that I simply needed to trust the process.

There *were* glimpses of light though, and a strong feeling of being at home in my true Self, as I delved into the deeper mysteries of life. My steady focus, and relentless work with my own development, led to quite a fast progress in grasping the psychology behind the different facets of my personality. I had many insights about the correlation between colors and visual fabric patterns with feelings and attitudes. As I saw how they could be used to balance the different parts of the psyche, I began to use them as tools to design my own identity.

Slowly I created a new life for myself. I really *had* developed a different way of working with clothes and started to teach others how to use colors, fabric patterns and garment styles on their path to inner balance and wholeness through talks, workshops and coaching. I also wrote my first book about this new way of looking at clothes and there were frequent magazine articles about me and my work.

As this new professional platform began to take shape, some began to approach me as an authority in my field. In a way I really was, which felt satisfying, but there was also hesitation. Or was it fear? It felt as if I risked becoming trapped by what I was in the process of building, trapped by people's projections of who they wanted me to be. Set in a form that would prevent me from continuing to go deeper in the exploration of my intriguing subject. Or was this fear about something else? I wasn't sure. Still, these doubts lead me to once again leave a promising career.

I left Stockholm, with all its professional opportunities, and set down new tentative roots in the wild woods further north. It felt like the perfect place to go deeper. But life had a surprise for me. My beloved daughter announced her arrival, which shifted my focus. I became more grounded. A few years on I found work as a teacher of textile craft while launching a collection in a very small scale. But another unexpected turn of events changed everything yet again. My daughter's father suddenly died, and financial circumstances forced me to leave the deep northern woods and move back to Stockholm to try to create a more stable situation.

There were certainly times when I was convinced that the job I had somehow "signed up for" was too big for me to handle. Sometimes I also questioned my choices. Maybe I could have compromised a little – stayed on my job as head of design while exploring what fascinated me on the side? But deep down I knew that a clean break had been necessary to make room for a totally different perspective. Even if I missed the big paycheck every month and the whole support system of a clothing company, I never really regretted my choice. Looking back I realized that the most important thing was that I followed my heart. Who knew where it would take me in the long run?

Since going back to fashion was unthinkable, I eventually began to work part time as a teacher of textile design while I kept exploring the deeper aspects of clothes. As my understanding grew, I wrote another book and gave an occasional talk. I also put a lot of work into creating collections for clothes and fabric patterns, but didn't have the financial means to launch them.

When my daughter left home a new period of my life started, that was basically filled with a small group of friends and my teaching work. But my heart wasn't really in it. Again there was this sense of a deep inner rumbling, telling me that something needed to change. Why didn't I work full time with what I knew was my true calling? Surely I could make it work if I put all my effort into it. I felt as if I just wasted my time unless I made a serious effort to contribute to change in the world of clothes in some way. Another bold career decision formed inside me and a few months later my teaching job came to an end.

My initial confidence, and what I had seen as freedom to follow my heart, gradually turned into despair as I became acutely aware of the grief, fear and rage that stood in my way and stopped me from fully expressing myself. In search for clarity I totally surrendered to face whatever blocked me, and was drawn into yet another dark night of the soul – this time even deeper and more scary than the first one. Inspired by *The Myth of Inanna* as she steps down to the underworld and stands naked before her neglected sister, I found myself in a process of stripping down to figurative nakedness. It felt like an absolute necessity in order to move past the obstacles to embody my inner Self and find an outer shape that was as genuine and transparent as it could be. Again my focus was this enigma of identity, so closely connected to the clothes we put around us.

I slowly found clarity through the practice of writing my book *Feminine Threads*, where I looked back at my own life journey and wove it all together. When I eventually returned to everyday life and ordinary awareness, it was with a more peaceful sense of being on a path of becoming who I was meant to be. However long it would take.

The two "dark" periods of my life, when the seams of my figurative garments burst open, were truly painful and deeply confusing. But they were also invaluable, since they came with the gift of a personal experience of the connection between the human identity process and clothes. My first crisis helped me understand the personality in all its aspects. I grew from being influenced by collective ideals to becoming aware of, and learning how to balance, the different facets of my psyche. I become more whole. The second shifted my focus from a fairly integrated personality to a deeper identification with my soul and feminine spirit, and the need to fully embody it. I still would not claim that my 2nd skin expresses my core being. It's a process and processes never really end. What matters is staying on the path.

A Meta Morphosis

T he word *metamorphosis* always had a specific meaning for me. Part of the reason for my fascination might be because, as a designer, I am involved with the transformation of outer form. But there is also this deep wonder and curiosity about the evolution of human consciousness, along with an inner knowing that the hidden worlds of our collective subconscious are intricately connected to how things are designed. The outer form simply has to change along with inner development.

If we take the word apart *meta* is Greek for beyond or transcending. This abstract perspective helps us look at an occurrence from an higher, overall perspective. The *morphosis* part of the word is about the various stages of the transformation, as well as the shifting of its outer form. This is exactly what *Bursting at the Seams* is about – an overall perspective of human transformation and how this affects and changes the outer form, which in this context refers to the clothes we wear.

As human beings on this planet we call Earth we are not equipped with fur, feathers or some kind of shell to protect our bodies. Since our skin is sensitive we create a 2nd skin with different kinds of materials and garments. We live in bodies that are designed to grow and as we mature, or gain weight, we get to experience this growth in a palpable way. We know how it feels when our body expands to a point when our clothes become too small. A natural growth process cannot be stopped, so unless our garments are replaced with a newer version that will fit, our movements will become limited and the seams will begin to burst.

The seed to this book came to me as an image of bursting seams while I pondered the effects of growth on an inner level – something that is built into our human design. In this process our way of perceiving who we are goes through a shift. As this happens our relationship to clothes, as well as how we express ourselves through them, needs to change accordingly. *Bursting at the Seams* explores this intimate relationship between our evolving Self and the dressed body and addresses questions like: What is human growth? What happens when we develop? What would "a larger version" of the clothes we wear really mean and how would they look? And how would this change the clothing industry?

Many animals shed an outer skin or shell at a specific point in their lives. Having reached a state where their inside can no longer fit into the existing form, it crawls out of the old, limiting parts. A new skin or shell develops.

Maybe the most radical, and definitely the most inspiring, is the metamorphosis of the caterpillar, since it so thoroughly changes what it is, as well as how it moves around and perceives the outer world. Initially the caterpillar is a creature who takes tiny steps on the ground. At a certain stage it begins to eat greedily and then, as on a given signal, it starts to create a chrysalis around itself. Inside of it the caterpillar's body digests itself. It is broken down into a new breed of cells called *imaginal cells*, that have the ability to become any type of cell. These begin to cluster to form this new creature, the butterfly, ready to experience life from a higher vantage point. What is really interesting is that the caterpillar and the butterfly have the exact same DNA. The only difference is that the cells begin to respond to a different set of organizing signals.

We might marvel at the transformation of the butterfly,
but fail to see the beauty of our own.
Maya Angelou

Can we compare this creature's amazing way of adapting to growth to similar processes in the human psyche? Does our identity have the ability to transform to make room for, adapt to and embody a part of us that can experience things from a higher vantage point?

As we open up to deeper levels of identification with our Self, Essence or Soul, contemporary Western clothing, as well as our relationship to them, really *do* begin to limit us. They cannot make room for the full expression of who we are, nor meet all our different needs. But like so many other creatures on our beautiful planet we can shed our 2nd skin, along with old identity layers, and create a new where there is room for larger parts of who we are.

Integrating Perspectives

Through this book's meandering path of exploring the intricate relationship between clothes and human growth, we will travel through outdated ideals and beliefs that hold us back. The combination of topics might be surprising. How can prehistoric cultural shifts, various psychological models or the inherent symbolism of shapes be relevant to the kind of garments we wear?

We need to search wide and deep to find the core issues behind the challenges we face today. On our explorative path we will switch between different lenses. A wide angle lens helps us zoom out to gain an overall view of how our culture has developed into what it is today.

There is a close relationship between clothes and culture. Clothes are *culture bearers*. Every era has told its story and shared its beliefs, ideals and attitudes through codes in the visual language of clothing. What was most highly valued in a specific culture and time period? How did they relate to gender? It's all there in the design and expression of their clothes. Colors, shapes, patterns and fabrics are mixed to express the subtle qualities of the *zeitgeist* – the spirit of the time – which is quite impossible to express in words. This does not mean that we will focus on the history of costume (there are other great books about that). It is simply a reminder of the close connection between these two subjects.

The human mind has been trained
to forget multidimensionality.
Our soul never forgets it.

As we zoom out, and merge different fields of knowledge, we will hopefully gain a new awareness of the reasons behind the emergence of values, ideals and beliefs. Since they are still present today as hidden drives behind fashion and dress codes, these need to be scrutinized.

A macro lens will be used to zoom in on inner levels so that we can take a closer look at human consciousness and the processes that help us evolve. An understanding of the development of the human identity, and how our needs shift through different evolutionary stages, will reveal the importance of a new take on clothing design.

As we zoom in we will also focus on our personal path. We already know that a garment helps us express personal characteristics. But our 2nd skin also functions as a *shaper of identity*, that helps mold our expanding identity. Since the different colors and patterns of the garments we wear influence our energy and thus our actions, this 2nd skin is also a *shape shifter*. This gives our garments a new importance, which will most probably change our clothing habits. Our relationship to clothes also changes when a different human need begins to motivate us.

Bursting at the Seams is an attempt to reconnect all these scattered threads of knowledge and perspectives into a whole, so that we can gain a deeper understanding of the garments we put around us. I firmly believe that there cannot be any real progress in the arena of clothing until we do.

PART I

Common Threads

If you change the way you look at things
the things you look at change.
Wayne Dyer

So why are the seams of our clothes bursting, figuratively speaking? In what way have they become too small for us? And if they are too small, why haven't we already made garments that fit us better?

Our ways of designing, manufacturing as well as relating to the clothes we wear are so intertwined with culture and human development that they cannot be separated from larger cultural forces at play. Renewal and transformation in the world of clothes need to go hand in hand with a shift of our dominant belief systems and mindsets.

Since there is a lot to explore regarding our common threads, this part has been divided into three sections. In *The Worn-Out Story* we begin by looking at the present state of our world, as well as the clothing industry. What values is our collective narrative built upon, how has it affected the system behind clothes and how is this belief system changing?

Our cultural roots might not be what we believed them to be. We take a deep dive back in time in *Where Did We Come From?* to trace our common threads through some larger twists and turns that seemed to shape the beliefs and mindsets of Western civilization. Exploring this question might provide clues as to why we find ourselves in critical times.

In *Culture as a Shaping Mold* we look at how the evolution of written language has shaped our consciousness along with our perception of identity. We also explore the origins or Western beauty ideals and compare them to those of other cultures.

In The Midst of a Shift

T he society we were born into forms like a giant hidden root system that we are all intricately interconnected with. Since we are parts of this larger whole we find our social belonging through its values, attitudes, morality, laws and specific ways of looking at, and understanding, life. This belief system is usually referred to as a cultural narrative or a paradigm. We can also call it the "Story" that helps us know what is real and important, and that brings meaning to the world we see around us. This Story has shaped all the different sectors of our society. Since it also affects the way we think and act, it even tells us who we are.

A Story is not obvious and easily translated into words since it is part of our collective subconscious. It is rather revealed through the under-lying values our societal structures have been built upon. Most of all we see it through its effects, like our ways of solving problems. Symbols and images in art and design, movie plots, as well as architectural structures, also help make it visible.

Contrary to systems that are alive and dynamic, those born out of our prevailing Story are quite closed, with static conditions and very little movement. Reality is based on certain mental filters, while some "truths" have been cemented. The reason for many of the challenges we face today is that this Story is beginning to lose its relevance. Its perspectives and mindsets are becoming outdated and are fast becoming an Old Story that no longer supports regeneration and beneficial growth.

We are in the midst of a shift between Stories. This "space in between" is an intermediate chaos of sorts, where our world is dangerously out of balance. Media tells us about natural disasters and health crises, about polarization and war. There is a crisis in economy, politics and education. The gap between the rich and the poor increases. Public health is plummeting. Life forms are dying out and our eco system is totally out of balance, which might threaten our very survival.

All of this seems to confirm that the world we are accustomed to is coming apart at the seams. This state of disintegration (similar to that of the caterpillar inside the chrysalis) produces fear which, by some, is dealt with by trying to hold on, even more tightly, to habitual ways of thinking and control things. If we are deeply rooted in the Old Story it can be really scary. We might stick our heads in the sand and go on as usual, with the result of extreme disconnect. We can blame the government, other countries or races, or a secret group of manipulators for the things that have gone wrong, which usually leads to resentment and victimhood. If we dare look deeper we can easily get confused about who and what to trust, since there is such complexity and so many different "truths" out there.

> A new world is emerging before our eyes.
> At the same time, the unsustainable world of the past struggles to continue.
> Both worlds reflect the beliefs that made them possible.
> Both worlds still exist - but only for now.
> *Gregg Braden*

Since "the old limiting shell" – of behavior patterns, practices and societal structures – needs to burst open, the journey from an old to a new Story might not be an easy ride, where we can just sit back and watch the metamorphosis of the world around us. Conflicts that have been buried need to rise to the surface to be acknowledged and healed in mutual respect. Fundamental assumptions that lie at the core of our culture, along with ingrained behaviors, need to be questioned and changed.

This shift challenges us to explore a new level of understanding. As we look beyond the obvious, it becomes clear that the crises we are facing is not about our economy, societal systems or the environment. There is not really a crisis in the clothing industry either. Our problems are the result of something that goes deeper – a Worn-Out Story. The simple truth is that we need a New Story.

When new perspectives emerge they are usually first disregarded, ridiculed and at times even demonized by the establishment. During a period of transition two Stories can exist simultaneously as polarized forces, with heated debates between them. But as a New Story gains acceptance, our world view and thinking patterns begin to change. We get to witness creative new ways of solving things, along with the regeneration of systems and practices in different areas of society.

> All truth passes through three stages.
> First, it is ridiculed.
> Second, it is violently opposed.
> Third, it is accepted as being self-evident.
> *Arthur Schopenhauer*

This way of looking at cultural transformation is the standard definition of a paradigm shift, and it seems obvious that we are in the midst of this process. Alternative views are often ridiculed and maligned. There is definitely growing polarization as well as heated conflicts. But even though the Old Story struggles to keep its footing, we can sense that something new and exciting is also beginning to take shape. Instead of being upset, scared or sad about what is falling apart, we can change our attitude to one of excitement about what is emerging. We can choose to see our present multi-crisis as an evolutionary driver to a whole new way of understanding the world, that will affect every aspect of life.

Something that forces us to use our power to develop ways to live that are truly sustainable.

There is no way to control or stop evolution. We can only participate in it. The most crucial changes of pushing on to higher levels of awareness take place in the realm of human consciousness. This means that the smoothness, duration and outcome of this shift depends on how well we embrace our role as active participants and take ownership of our part in it. We have all been involved in upholding the Story our society is built upon. Acknowledging that we are part of the problem automatically makes us part of the solution. This is huge, since it gives us back our power.

The transformation of the whole rest upon the integration of the unique individual cells. This tells us that changing beliefs and mindsets, resolving our conflicts and integrating polarities, is a process that takes place inside each one of us. As cells in a bigger whole even our thoughts, feelings and state of mind have an impact. When we raise our self awareness, and open up to new possibilities, the world changes with us. We literally become the imaginal cells inside our collective chrysalis.

What is important to remember though, is that the logic of the Old Story does not apply in the New Story. Wings are something *totally* unfathomable to a caterpillar, so in order to perceive new perspectives we need to embrace the unknown and trust our intuition. As imaginal cells we all need to listen, with sharp attention, to the new organizing signals that help us move on to a new stage of evolution.

Hacking Fashion

T he values and morality of our Old Story, as well as its specific ways of looking at life, has shaped Western civilization as well as the system behind the clothing industry. So what are those values? What are the mechanics behind this system and the fuel that keeps it running? To find out we need to hack fashion.

Quite a few years ago I wrote this passage in my notebook: "Am I one of a group of system busters on a mission to enter into the system of fashion, figure out the mechanics behind it, leave it and then bust it!" The thought appealed to me as much as it amused me. I had never felt like an ordinary designer anyway. Regardless of how much I enjoyed creating beautiful fabrics and clothes, it was never enough to fill my longing for a deeper purpose and the future oriented drive that came with it. Everything I had studied, practiced and experienced regarding the design, production and marketing of clothes fell into place and became so very obvious from the vantage point of being a fashion hacker.

What comes to mind for most people who hear the word hacking is hidden culprits who use their technical skills to break into computer networks, personal accounts or digital devices to access sensitive data, corrupt a system and introduce malware. But the basic definition of hacking is merely to enter and explore a system with the intention of figuring out the codes and processes that drives it. There is nothing bad about that. Benevolent hackers help companies improve their systems.

Bio-hackers explore the different systems in our bodies to search for life styles that can optimize them. If we discover the dynamics behind the garment and fashion industry we should be able to use this knowledge to bypass its challenges.

Everything we do in the world is infused with our present state of consciousness and the way we understand life. This is why the systems we have created are literally a manifestation of the prevalent Story. So if the industry behind clothing has a limited knowledge of the close connection between our evolving human identity and the clothes we wear, it will affect design concepts and how these are marketed. A lack of understanding of our dependence on the natural world will set the tone for how clothing production is managed and how goods are transported. So even though beginning to use organic fabrics is a really good thing, it doesn't change the foundation of the system.

> The way we see the world
> shapes the way we relate to it.
> If a mountain is a deity, not a pile of ore.
> If a forest is a sacred grove, not timber.
> If other species are biological kin, not resources.
> If the planet is our mother, not an opportunity.
> Then we will treat each other with greater respect.
> Thus is the challenge, to look at the world
> from a different perspective.
> *David Suzuki*

Even though fashion is built on changes of style, the system behind it isn't built to adapt to any real change. Its purpose is to keep functioning in predictable patterns that are continuously repeated. It is organized to maneuver things so that they are controllable. This means that even when we begin to understand the negative effects of the system it can be difficult, and maybe even impossible, to integrate major change. We need to begin by scrutinizing the very ideas behind its construction. If the system behind clothes and fashion has no room for changing human values and emerging needs in a time of rapid change, it might be time to seriously question it. Maybe it has served its purpose.

Even though nothing is set in this intriguing space in between cultural narratives, the time for a New Story of clothes is definitely approaching. When our paradigm changes an entirely new system needs to be created, one that is based on an expanded perspective of our human journey. Let's begin by exploring the drivers behind our present clothing system. This seems crucial in order to grasp why it has such a powerful grip on us.

A System of Waste

Around 300 years ago our ways of looking at consumption, work and wealth began to change along with the realization that economic growth can be manipulated. If more was wanted by people, more could be produced and wealth would be accumulated. When the industrial revolution occurred at the end of the eighteenth century, modern capitalism was born and spread throughout western Europe. Capitalism is still one of the dominant drivers behind the clothing industry.

This development transformed the clothing industry in just one century, from custom-made to mass production, with standardized sizes and styles for immediate purchase. New materials for clothes, made of synthetic fibers, were also introduced, which made it possible to offer affordable garments that were also very easy to wash and dry. These significant changes were brought about by technological advances as well as social and cultural changes. Along with the concept of fashion seasons and trend cycles – a development that was driven by the rise of fashion magazines – the influence of designers also grew.

The clothing industry is huge, with an estimated value of $1.79 trillion in 2024. It is also one of the dirtiest global industries, in more ways than one, that reflects our contemporary values, as well as weaknesses, like no other.

Let's remind ourselves of some of the facts:

- Fast fashion and online shopping has made clothes even less expensive and easier to buy, so our appetite for new clothes has grown rapidly. After taking a hit in 2020 due to the Covid-19 pandemic, the markets have recovered and thrived with people buying 60% more clothes than they did a couple of decades ago.

- The garments produced each year is said to have surpassed 100 billion in 2014. The estimates vary between 80 and 150 billion, but the numbers seem impossible to verify. According to *Fashion Revolution's Transparency Index 2023*, a stunning 88% of 250 of the world's largest brands don't disclose their annual product volumes.

- If we compare an estimate of 100 billion garments a year to a global population of 8,2 billion, the numbers are truly shocking.

- The available statistics suggest that 10 - 40% of the garments that are produced every year are not sold, which is an enormous waste of resources. Unwanted garments are instead donated to charities, which might be fine if they were valued and used. But they are not. Most of them end up in landfills, with dire consequences to the environment. Unsold stock is even burnt, which further damages our eco-system.

- Only 1% of the clothes made are recycled into new textiles or garments. 12% is down-cycled into something of lesser value. 87% of textile waste is pure loss.

- The clothing industry causes huge amounts of carbon emission, soil and water pollutants. It is one of the biggest polluters on the planet. According to the organization Fashion Revolution most brands will need to reduce emissions by at least 90% to reach net-zero. Their report *What Fuels Fashion* found that the emissions of 42 brands have actually increased.

- More than two-thirds of the clothes manufactured are made from petroleum based polymers, commonly known as plastic. The fibers are turned into synthetic materials such as polyester, spandex, acrylic, elastane and nylon. These materials shed micro-plastics when we wash them and huge amounts of them find their way to our oceans. Nobody really knows how this will affect our ecosystem or us, but it is obviously not a good thing.

- Even though fabrics made from natural materials – like linen, wool, hemp or cotton – don't shed microplastics, the large amounts of chemicals, dyes and detergents used in their production has a negative impact on the environment, as well as on their ability to biodegrade.

- Materials such as viscose, Modal, Lyocell and Tencel are semi-synthetic, since they also have natural origins. Compared to synthetic alternatives these are more environmentally friendly, but large amounts of chemicals are needed to make them into fibers.

- The extensive use of chemicals and toxins used in textile and garment manufacturing are left in the clothes, even after several washes. As we wrap our bodies in these garments our skin absorbs them, which has a negative impact on our health.

- A majority of textile and garment workers can hardly afford to live in decent housing, eat healthy food, go to the doctor or send their kids to school.

Big brands are clinging to their toxic relationship with fossil fuels
and it's not just plastic-based fibers and fabrics.
Fossil fuels are found throughout the entire fashion supply chain;
they are in every stitch of our wardrobes.
Fashion Revolution

Most of us are aware of these problems and their many negative consequences. A large number of clothing companies are also doing admirable work to improve the methods and processes that harm our natural environment as well as conditions for textile workers. New policies are made in EU making producers, fashion brands and retailers responsible for the entire lifecycle of textiles. As consumers we try to be more conscious of which textile materials to use, buy more secondhand and choose the sustainable options that are offered when we do buy something new.

But when the question of sustainability is raised, there is an exaggerated focus on materials and production methods. Is organic cotton better than lyocell? Can we keep using polyester if it is recycled, if we use filters in our washing machines? Sure, using materials that are good for the environment, as well as for people, is as important as raising the quality of clothing production. But it isn't enough. It's like focusing on treating some of the obvious symptoms, while closing our eyes to forces at play beneath the surface.

Outdated Mindsets

So what are these symptoms saying about our present culture? Christine Wamsler is a professor of sustainability science at Lund University. According to her what lies at the heart of climate change, and the sustainability challenges we face today, is the human mindset. She compares it to an iceberg. What is above the water are the events and crises we are aware of. Hidden below the water are our mindsets and patterns of behavior that, in the end, lead to the events and crises that we see on top of the iceberg.

> The world as we have created it is a process of our thinking.
> It cannot be changed without changing our thinking.
> *Albert Einstein*

So what mindsets have lead to all these negative consequences? Which beliefs, values and ideals can be found in the submerged part of our fashion iceberg?

An Illusion of Separation

At the core of the Old Story there is separation – humanity from nature, me from you, inner from outer. This mindset underlies all of the symptoms of our metacrisis, and is part of the foundation for every societal institution. It even governs our sense of identity. It's as if we believe that we are the center of everything and that the rest of the world is something "out there". The English writer, speaker and philosopher Alan Watts called this *The Skin-Encapsulated Ego* – a sense of absolute separateness from everything else. What is inside the skin is 'me', what is outside is 'not me'.

This is an illusion. In reality we cannot separate ourselves from the rest of creation. We are part of it. Simply becoming aware of this is not enough to heal the illusion, though. We need to remember who we are beneath the Story and its mindsets, and feel our deep connection to natural life and the rest of the world.

Fragmentation

Fragmentation is a powerful mindset. The split up parts end up in separate compartments, resulting in little or no connection between various fields of knowledge or experiences. In health care, for instance, there are heart experts, specialists in nutrition and psychology, but an interaction between these fields is rare, even though it might support a more permanent healing for the patient. While scientists have a deep and complex understanding of one small piece of the whole, how the fragmented pieces fit together doesn't seem as interesting. We can make similar observations in other fields, like in the school system where there is rarely any connection between different subjects.

So how does this relate to clothing? The production of a garment is fragmented into many different steps where no one is responsible for the entire process. Instead of giving a garment style a long life where improvements to optimize its functions are made when needed, they usually only see the light of day during one collection or season. The sizes and shapes of our physical bodies have been split up into standardized measurements. Instead of relating to our identity as a complex, integrated whole, with a unique mix of characteristics, it has been divided into different parts, or styles – one for work, one for leisure or celebrations, etc. Our surface persona (the garments we use) has been disconnected from our inner worlds and the constant movement and expansion of our identity. As long as these inner parts are subdued (like in the iceberg analogy) our focus stays on surface levels.

Loss of Synergy

Separation and fragmentation results in a loss of synergy. Every whole is composed of unique parts, with equal value as well as a specific purpose. But reality cannot be reduced to these smaller units. It is the system as a whole that determines how the parts behave.

Whether we look at an oak tree, some kind of mold, a specific culture or a human being, the one thing that is crucial is synergy. In any successfully working organism the different parts are in harmony with the whole and function together in a natural and spontaneous way. Our own body is a perfect example. If synergy drops and the organism does not receive the support of its many parts, it becomes ill. If it drops altogether the body dies. A social group functions in the same way. High in synergy means there is a low grade of conflict. Our civilization, along with our systems, is obviously in a state of low synergy.

A lack of Love and Respect for Nature

Large parts of the clothing industry is built on a lack of care and responsibility for its impact on our environment. The way we pollute nature by dumping toxins and waste, as well as how we waste our natural resources like there is no limit, all come down to one mindset: We don't truly value and respect nature. As Stella McCartney so graphically described it: "The fashion industry rapes the land on a daily basis."

We might see ourselves as lovers of nature, but as long as we keep buying lots of new clothes, while closing our eyes to the dire consequences of the industry, we are part of this mindset. As we all know this mindset doesn't just apply to the clothing industry. It permeates our culture.

The Value of a Garment

The reduced value of clothes is closely tied to the development of the textile industry. New ways of manufacturing garments were developed where the production process was split up into different work stages. Labor saving machinery was introduced and the work was streamlined to make clothes cheaper. As profit began to trump quality, the value of cloth and clothing changed dramatically.

If we know the time and skills needed to cut and sew a shirt, knit a sweater or weave a fabric, we understand how ridiculous the prices of fast fashion, and most clothes, are. Textiles used to be highly valued (and still are in some cultures). Not so long ago fabrics and garments were seen as treasures to pass on to younger generations. When I grew up it was a given to use hand-me-down clothes from my older sister. It was also still a common tradition in Sweden to prepare a hope chest with handwoven towels, embroidered sheets and tablecloths for the young women of the family, to eventually start their own homes. Nowadays people usually look for bargains. Even if there are machines to weave the fabric, it needs to be dyed, cut, sewn, packed and transported around the world.

> The price of clothes may be low
> but they are paid for with human lives.
> *Katharine Hamnett*

There is also the other end of the continuum – the exaggerated value of designer items. Yes, the quality is higher, but we also pay for the brand. We strive to identify with those that are raised in esteem, and in the world of clothes and fashion this can be translated to designer items.

Lack of Respect for Humans

One thing that we already touched upon is the exploitation of textile workers. But isn't there also a lack of respect for human individuality?

We are all unique and have different needs, so why should we try to fit into standard measurements? Readymade sizes don't fit everyone since many are taller, thinner, larger or smaller. Shouldn't clothes be made to fit us and not the other way around?

Human health is also often disregarded in the race for profit. As we dress from head to toe in inexpensive clothes, we are often exposed to dangerous chemicals. How many know that quite a low percent of the clothes we buy are free of toxins? Parts of the textile industry is thus built on a lack of responsibility as well as lack of care for human life.

A Habit of Conforming

One thing that stands out when it comes to mindsets is our tendency to conform. We look to media, trend setters and influencers, or anyone who is raised to a high status in the public eye, to show us the silent language of success through their outfits. This drive to conform – which is like handing over the authority of our choices to somebody else – is a widespread pattern in our culture and a habit we rarely seem to question. We simply trust the authority to decide for us. In school we learn what we are told is important and have no real power to change the curriculum. Media chooses which news we get to hear about, in a way that can be biased. Even if fashion brands cannot force us to buy certain garments, it definitely narrows down our choices, since trends control which styles and colors end up in clothing stores. Many try to fit into the same mold – to look the same and think according to the prevailing belief system. It's as if we are asked to follow a path laid out for us by whomever, or whatever, has been appointed our collective authority.

This path of conforming is so engrained that if you question it, or don't conform, you might be seen as radical or rebellious. Not in fashion though. This is one of the few places where being different can be idolized. Maybe the reason as to why a clothing rebel is accepted, appreciated and even seen as someone to follow, is because it is a kind of rebellion that doesn't challenge our belief system in any outspoken way.

How did we get lured into this pattern of listening to somebody else instead of following our own taste and inclination, our own heart and guts? As human beings our true strength depends on us all being unique parts of a multi-faceted whole. We *don't* look the same nor think the same. This is one enigma we will explore in later chapters.

A Belief in Perpetual Growth

One of the primary drivers behind Western culture is a belief in the value of economic growth. When this mindset is prioritized it leads to a never-ending race for profit. Aggressive marketing leads to a growing demand that speeds up the cycle of new collections. Time becomes an important factor that gets juggled and squeezed in this pursuit. Short lead times are made possible through worse conditions for laborers. Corners might be cut to get the garments to consumers as fast as possible. The result is garments of bad quality that are easily damaged after a few wears or washes, and thus easily trashed. As a consequence we soon need new clothes again.

The size of an economy is typically measured by the production of goods and services, and according to many experts economic growth is a good thing. But doesn't this mean that we need to consume even more goods and services? That the growth of our economy actually depends on if we stop cooking for ourselves, distance ourselves from our personal connection to the clothes we wear, and pay for somebody else to take care of our children? If we share this belief we need to keep handing over the responsibility to choose styles, materials and ways to produce our garments to the clothing industry, instead of making, mending and swapping clothes, and recognize the value of high quality garments that can be worn for decades. Sure, there are more complex issues related to the economy of a country, like employment rates, taxes and societal services, but when is it enough? This is one of the beliefs we need to question.

Toxic cycles of overconsumption

We already know about the consequences when costumers are lured into an exaggerated consumption. Heaps of clothes are gathered which fast become outdated. This, in turn, pushes us to replace them with something new.

> Solutions are not outside of ourselves
> they live within the wounds that we have.
> *Zach Bush*

As we look at these different mindsets and their underlying values it becomes obvious how interrelated they are. How one leads to another. The impossibility of knowing which came first. If we truly loved nature we would value its resources. Toxic waste would be unheard of. Respect for human lives would be self-evident, which would mean that things the exploitation of textile laborers would be unthinkable. Chemicals that might damage our health would not be used. Overconsumption would not exist without a belief in economic growth. Fashion would not even be a word without a polarized view where styles (along with attitudes) are over- or undervalued. If we were not stuck in an illusion of separation none of the things mentioned would exist.

All of these mindsets are part of the Worn-Out Story. To find their roots we need to look beyond the veils of our cultural heritage. But before we do, let's look briefly at one quite interesting primary driver.

Redirecting Growth

We already know that our consumer patterns have spun out of control. We seem culturally obsessed to acquire things, become bored with them and then dump them. At the core of the complex pattern behind perpetual growth, overconsumption and waste, there is a common denominator that, at first glance, looks like blind and self-serving greed.

But how did we become these beings, with elaborately decorated surfaces, that seem to hide a hollow hole of hunger on the inside – much like the earthbound caterpillar who is craving more and more to eat? It's as if we're trying to satisfy some need, but no matter how much we consume the need does not get met. It almost seems like an addiction. If we treated it as such it would be imperative to examine the hidden, underlying driving force in order to understand it.

What if we cannot and shouldn't even try to stop this impulse? Maybe this craving for more isn't inherently bad, but rather an innate aspect of human nature, a healthy impulse for growth with an evolutionary purpose? A drive that should simply be redirected? Growth is, in its essence, a natural urge for expansion that helps us evolve as a species as well as individuals.

In order for this growth to be beneficial though, we need to change our focus from outer to *inner* expansion and development. Like our caterpillar we need some time inside a symbolic chrysalis to look inwards. In this process our perspective is shifted from outer expansion of our wardrobe, and economic growth that only serves a few, to human and cultural growth that will change the conditions into something better for us all. Central in this redirection from outer to inner is figuring out what natural development this expansive force is aiming for. This is our true challenge.

Our path forward might not be to try to fix the cracks in the foundation of a failing system. It could rather be to question the mindsets that built it and lay the groundwork for a new system made of a different set of values such as transparency, integrity and a shared commitment to the greater good. One where we become regenerators rather than consumers.

THE WORN-OUT STORY

Asking the Right Questions

E arly on, as I pondered how clothes could be designed to be truly beneficial to the wearer, a few fundamental questions stood out as crucial:

Who are we?
To even begin to grasp how clothes could be designed in a way that would be good for us, I needed to learn more about the psyche and what forces that shape our inner worlds. Understanding the difference between parts of us like Self, personality, ego, as well as their functions, seemed like necessary basic knowledge. Would I, for instance, be able to design cutlery if I was unfamiliar with the consistency of porridge, vegetables or meat? Most probably I wouldn't do a good job.

What forces drive human evolution?
I already knew that what we need from clothes, as well as our motivation to wear them, changes throughout life. We rarely use the same type of garments at 50 as we do in adolescence, so it was obvious that our needs develop along with age. But do our needs also change as we grow and mature on an inner level? I soon discovered that there certainly are different stages of inner growth.

Understanding the evolutionary forces behind these seemed essential to learn how clothes could help us fill the needs that came along with them.

Where did we come from and how did we get here?

Do we really know who we are if we don't know our past? Can we have a clear vision of where we are going if we are not aware of our history and previous mistakes?

In school we are taught that Western civilization began about 5,500 years ago in Sumer and Egypt. But is that really the full story? New discoveries prove that we are part of a much older, and in many respects more advanced, civilization. These missing pieces might help us better understand our human evolution.

What kind of future do we want to create?

A part of me was convinced that our civilization would go through fundamental changes during my lifetime. If it was true, this meant that we would most probably be challenged to make important choices regarding our future.

The answers to the questions above might provide a deeper understanding, help us find new solutions to existing problems and restructure systems as well as practices.

The Cultural Backdrop

A s humans we are immensely creative. Our feats are truly marvelous. Comparing how we live today to a couple of hundred years ago is inspiring, to say the least. Looking at how we can now communicate easily and travel comfortably all over the world, or just ordinary things like all the different kinds of food that are available in stores today, is mind-blowing. But even though our intentions behind all this progress might have been good, we didn't foresee some of the consequences. It actually seems like many of the cultural advances also contain the seeds of our demise.

> The past is destined to be the future
> unless we understand it.
> *Billy Carson*

In order to leave the Worn-Out Story, that we seem so stuck in as a culture, and create a New Story, we need to understand how we got to where we are. As we shed light upon the somewhat tilted perspective we seem to have of our common past, and question the accepted definition of an advanced culture, our awareness regarding what kind of foundation our culture is built upon grows. So does our understanding of how these cultural roots have shaped human consciousness and modern life. Knowing more about the development of culture might also help us understand why the prevalent modern needs, that most of us can easily relate to, became part of our everyday lives and even shaped how clothes are used and designed.

The reason for this exploration of Western culture is to better understand how our Old Story emerged. Which forces shifted our sense of identity to the fragmented and separated state we find ourselves in? What kind of evolution shaped modern civilization? In search for the origins of our present dilemma, and the somewhat shady unspoken rules of our culture, we might find some valuable clues.

Even though it can seem far-fetched to delve into ancient cultures in a book with clothes as its main focus, I believe it is necessary. The drivers behind our way of using garments, as well as how our human identity has been shaped over millennia, are so intimately intertwined with culture. So let's trace the frayed and hidden threads that connect us to our deepest shared roots — which are, after all, the strongest and most vital — and look at the twists and turns that shaped the destiny of Western civilization.

Hidden Stories

Ancient culture is like a huge tapestry. Many threads are still visible and clearly expressed through colors and shapes that we can easily see and interpret. But it's not the full story. Some threads have deteriorated and are lost forever. Others are unseen. But they are still there, concealed behind its surface. As the hidden side of the tapestry is laid bare, with all its knots and partly broken threads, secrets about a forgotten past are open for all to see. Without these, our story is incomplete.

Our greatest challenge in trying to fill in the gaps and reimagine the specific patterns of this tapestry is not about the missing threads, though. It's the automatic assumptions and unconscious biases that are part of our Old Story. As long as we are set in this narrative, believing we already know what's there, our minds are forever closed to new information.

Sumer, in the historical region of southern Mesopotamia, is commonly regarded as "the cradle of Western civilization". It began to take form in the 4th millennium BC and the general belief is that it was here, along with ancient Egypt, that the earliest scripts (and thus the first historical records) were developed around 3,400-3,200 BC.

But what is a civilization? Scholars have defined it by criteria such as the formation of settlements with public buildings and social structures, a non-nomadic population, monumental architecture, the existence of social classes and the use of writing for communication, along with domesticated animals, agriculture, the development of techniques for pottery, weaving and metallurgy. But is a class-based society really an important criteria for a civilization? Does architecture have to be monumental? And how do we define writing?

We might associate ancient civilizations with Stonehenge, one of the most well-known prehistoric construction feats in human history. But when we begin to look at the physical evidence of earlier civilizations that are left around the world, there are much older marvels that bear testament to the skills and sophistication of our ancestors and provide glimpses into forgotten civilizations. The history we were taught in school simply cannot be the full picture. Most likely we have barely scratched the surface of understanding our common past.

What we find in Göbekli Tepe in southeastern Turkey, defies our traditional view of early humanity and prehistoric times. It is so old and complex that, based on common belief about the development of civilization, it shouldn't exist at all. Its construction dates back around 11,600 years, which means that it predates Stonehenge by 6,500 years and Sumer by around 5,000 years.

The site was first uncovered in the 1960s, but its significance wasn't truly realized until excavations began in 1996. Circles of massive T-shaped stone pillars were unearthed and more than 200 similar pillars in about 20 circles are known through geophysical surveys. Each has a height of up to 5,5 m (18 ft), weighs up to 15 tons and are fitted into sockets hewn out of local bedrock. Most of the central pillars are decorated with elaborate drawings of animals and some have intricate animal statues carved right onto the pillar's surface – a quality of art that stands out in comparison to the more primitive and commonly known cave paintings.

Our experts insist that hunter gatherers, who lived in simple mud huts, were the only humans that existed at this time. The wheel wasn't yet invented and horses were not tamed. Göbekli Tepe challenges these ideas. How could they have moved these gigantic stone pillars? And how would they have carved out elaborate images of animals without metal tools? The geometric precision found at the site indicates a knowledge of applied geometry far beyond its time. Even by modern standards it is a gigantic construction project, that wouldn't have been possible without some kind of organized and stable social structure already in place.

Early on Göbekli Tepe was believed to be a lone destination where nomadic people came to worship, but at least a dozen more sites from the same period have recently been identified in the hills nearby. One of them, Karahan Tepe, seems to be even older and includes residential areas with daily household items. All these sites form what is today known as Taş Tepeler, The Stone Hills culture, that existed between 12,000 – 8,000 BC in an area of some 200 kilometers. Even though only small parts have yet been uncovered, they shine new light upon the dawn of civilization.

Boncuklu Tarla is another site from a similar time period and area, where a large number of monumental architecture remains, along with private and public buildings, skeletal remains and many ornaments.

Every layer of earth that we peel back
brings us closer to uncovering the full tapestry
of our shared history.

These important pieces of evidence weren't unearthed until after World War II, when archaeology as a systematic inquiry into the life, thought, technology and social organization of our ancestors began to be more established. But the facts that have been unearthed clash with common belief about advanced cultures, which might explain why the obvious signs of ancient high level cultures seem downplayed and ignored. It might take time for the scientific community to accept this game-changing research, but it forces us to question our beliefs about the rise of Western culture.

The oldest records of our past, along with indigenous beliefs, support a cyclic view of the world, where civilizations rise and fall as a result of a destructive development or catastrophic events. The cold period of about 1,300 years, usually referred to as The Younger Dryas, is one of our most well-known examples of abrupt, catastrophic climate change. Its cause remained a mystery for a long time. One hypothesis suggests a massive flood of water (described in many ancient texts) in the western Arctic, another an asteroid or comet that hit the earth.

Regardless of which, this catastrophe didn't only lead to a long period of extremely cold weather, but also to the extinction of many animals and plants. Even though it also led to a serious decline in human populations, there were survivors. Some are believed to have migrated to the warmer climate in the Southern Hemisphere, while others might have sought refuge in a few hospitable areas or returned to a more nomadic lifestyle. A second abrupt climatic event, approximately 11,600 years ago, marked the end of the last ice age and the beginning of Earth's present climate.

Considering that The Stone Hills culture, as well as Boncuklu Tarla, seemed to have emerged at the time of this shift, could it represent a reboot that led to the rise of our present civilization? We can only speculate about the skilled beings who built them. Regardless of their origins, the fact that they were highly advanced means that they must have had a strong impact on what followed.

If these ancient cultures really *did* mark a kind of reboot of civilization, what values and beliefs can be seen in the time period that followed, the settlements that seem built by more ordinary people? What did life look like alongside and after The Stone Hills culture (that was, strange as it seems, buried on purpose around 8,000 BC) and up until the Sumerian civilization began to flourish around 4,000 BC? How did we relate to nature and the cosmos? What was the relationship between men and women like? The answers to those questions must tell us about a more Original Story.

A Very Different Culture

T he inhabitants of southeastern Europe and some parts of the Middle East were hardly primitive villagers at this time. They had varied crops, domesticated animals and specialized crafts. By 7,000 BC there was complex social organization as well as spiritual and governmental institutions. Technologies that supported and enhanced the quality of life were emphasized and people were already living in plastered brick houses, some with clay ovens and chimneys. There were innovations in town planning, development of tools and household articles. The arts flourished. Sailboats were used from 6,000 BC, which led to expanded trade and tremendous cross-fertilizing impetus to cultural growth. Practically all the material and social technologies that are fundamental to civilization, as well as a spiritual foundation, were in place.

In the absence of written texts (or rather records that are understood) most knowledge of prehistory and early civilizations are contained in archaeological findings. Through housing, city planning, symbols in art, graves and deities of worship, so much can be understood about the way our ancestors lived and interacted.

The discovery and excavation in the late 1950s of two neolithic sites, Çatalhöyük and Hacilar, situated in what is now modern Turkey, was a journey into this lost world and led to immeasurably increased knowledge of prehistory. Both showed remnants of a very different culture, with a stability and continuity of growth over several thousand years for a progressively more advanced culture.

Çatalhöyük, the largest of these two settlements, flourished around 7,000 BC. Even though only one twentieth of the site has been excavated, it is obvious that it was remarkably advanced. Buildings testify to the birth of architecture and conscious planning, its economy shows advanced practices in agriculture and stock-breeding, and its imports to a flourishing trade in raw materials. Art was also advanced and centered around a complex female symbolism. Numerous sanctuaries testify to a Goddess-worshipping mythology and religion.

No difference in wealth of equipment is discernible between male and female graves and there are no other marked distinctions based on either class or sex, or signs of the sexual inequality we have been taught is "human nature". There are obvious signs of an equalitarian, non-patriarchal society.

There is also an absence of fortification and thrusting weapons, and no signs of damage through warfare. This peaceful character is one of the most remarkable and thought-provoking features of The Old European civilizations – a term coined by the Lithuanian archaeologist Marija Gimbutas to describe a relatively homogeneous culture in Southeast Europe. They never seemed to settle in inconvenient places such as high and steep hills, which is seen later on as forts with stone walls were built. It seems like places were chosen for their beautiful setting, good water and soil, and plenty of animal pastures. Art shows that there's a concept of the cosmos, of the complementary roles of male and female, and a close relationship with nature.

The clear indication of peaceful and equalitarian social structures is still not the view of many scholars, though. Male dominance, along with private property and slavery, is still regarded as by-products of the agrarian revolution. New discoveries are usually interpreted with a bias of "primitive" man as bloodthirsty, warlike hunters and a slow progression of behavioral and cultural development.

Some claim that Old Europe was among the most sophisticated and advanced places in the world before the first cities emerged in Mesopotamia. At its peak around 5,000–3,500 BC it had developed many of the political, technological, and ideological signs of "civilization". Nothing points to hierarchies among social classes and the use of (our present definition of) written language, though. Some Old European villages grew to city-like sizes, larger than the earliest cities of Mesopotamia. These weren't just some cultural backwater, they might rather have been the true origin of our civilization.

The Mother Goddess

T he female images on wall paintings, in cave sanctuaries and burial sites, as well as the small sculptures carved out of stone or bone that are traditionally referred to as *Venus figurines*, have been found spread over a wide area – from the Balkans in Eastern Europe to Lake Baikal in Siberia, all the way west to Willendorf near Vienna and the Grotte du Pape in France. The oldest one found in Europe is 40,000 years old.

Some scholars saw them as an expression of male eroticism or barbaric images used in primitive fertility rites – interpretations that say more about the perceivers. Since they are so abundant, and so widespread, these female figurines cannot be dismissed that easily. We should rather assume that they are charged with a depth of meaning and tell us something that is central to our psychic heritage and the origins of human culture.

When the archaeological pioneer Marija Gimbutas first published findings from her own excavations, as well as from over three thousand other sites, no less than thirty thousand of these miniature sculptures had been uncovered. They are the most significant and expressive traces of ancient European culture and hint at a widespread worship of a female deity that would later develop into a complex spiritual concept.

The Mother Goddess incarnates the creative principle as *The Source and Giver of All*. She is a symbol of the unity of life in nature and the personification of all that is sacred and mysterious on Earth. This does not mean that earlier cultures were matriarchal. There is a multitude of evidence that these were based on equality and partnership. The social structure where one gender rules over the other was a result of the later dominator cultures. During earlier periods humans were not pre-occupied with warring gods and heroes. Gods and Goddesses were not perceived as rulers, kings or parents, but as personified forces of nature. The practice of spirituality seemed to focus on natural phenomena that helped us understand the world. The earliest myths were thus centered around the cycles of life and nature, and above all around the Great Mother – the origin of everything.

A Mother Goddess is known in all cultures, with different names, and is part of many belief systems. In myth and religion the term *Triple Goddess* has been used to refer to a single feminine deity as well as to a goddess triad, responsible for the eternal processes of life, death and rebirth. According to Marija Gimbutas, author of *Goddesses and Gods of Old Europe*, it is evident that the Triple Goddess was worshipped by the people of Old Europe before the patriarchal religions arrived.

In Greek mythology *The Moirae* personify the inescapable destiny of man and the fate of every person. They spun the metaphorical life threads of all living beings, even the gods, and cut them when they thought it was time. Clotho, "the spinner", spun the thread of life from her distaff onto her spindle. Lachesis, "the allotter", measured the thread of life allotted to each person with her measuring rod. Atropos, "the inexorable" or "inevitable", cut the thread of life with her "abhorred shears". A similar concept is found in Nordic mythology, where *The Norns* – Urd, Verdandi and Skuld – determined the destiny of all living beings by spinning the threads of life.

The threefold manifestation of the Goddess is also known as *The*

Maiden, Mother and Crone. Each symbolizes a separate stage in the female life cycle as well as a phase of the moon: The Maiden is inception, a promise of new beginnings, enchantment and youthful enthusiasm represented by the waxing moon. The Mother is ripeness, fertility, fulfillment, life and stability represented by the full moon. The Crone is wisdom, power, repose, endings and death represented by the waning moon.

While the Maiden and Mother are loved and respected archetypes in western culture, the Crone is not. If you look up the word in a dictionary the not-very-pleasant description says: "a witch-like, ugly and withered old woman". But the Crone hasn't always been seen this way. In the cultures or Old Europe, this archetype embodied feminine wisdom and great power.

A few ancient symbols – the Triquetra, the Triskele and the Trinacria – express and embody the wisdom of this feminine trinity. Even though the Triquetra, or Trinity Knot, is often seen as Celtic, its origins remain a mystery. Groups like the Celts, Wicca, Gauls, Scythians, Vikings and others, seem to have had interconnected ideas and traditions. Even though their languages and religions varied, the Triquetra has been found in vastly different tribes. Carved on the Newgrange Stone Monument and Indian heritage sites, engraved on everyday items like Norse saddles and combs, and on ancient pagan tombs that are thousands of years old. The concept of interconnectedness of natural forces and the eternal cycle of life seems to be the foundation for all these groups.

The Triskelion is known in Sicily as the Trinacria, a three-legged woman. It was adopted in 1282 as their symbol and became the official Sicilian flag in 1943. In the Trinacria a woman's head is at the center of the three legs and the symbols of wings, snakes and wheat are added. The head is said to represent Medusa, a beautiful Greek goddess who in the legend was raped in a temple and afterwards turned into a monster with snakes instead of hair. She was later beheaded by the young hero Perseus. The legend of this mythical figure seems to hold an important clue in the development of Western civilization.

The book *Female Rage: Unlocking its Secrets, Claiming its Power* by Mary Valentis and Anne Devane is partly based on interviews where women were asked what female rage looked like to them. What came to mind was always Medusa, the snaky-haired monster of myth. Even though none of the interviewed women could remember the details of the myth, a large number of women recognized this mythical figure as the face of women's rage over abuse and being robbed of power.

Robert Graves, an English poet and novelist who was well-known for his translations and interpretations of the Greek myths, believed that the myth about Medusa preserves the memory of the conflicts which occurred between men and women in the transition to a patriarchal society. To him the episode of Perseus' victory over Medusa represents the end of female ascendancy and the taking over of the temples by men.

> The Goddess myths are both our heritage and our future.
> They are the stories that tell us
> where we came from and what is possible.
> *Bonnie J. Horrigan*

Myth can shed light upon our ancient past and help us understand how Western culture evolved. In their book *Hel, the Hidden Goddess in Nordic Mythology*, Gunnel and Göran Liljeroth explore Norse mythology, its Mother Goddess and the people who lived with this concept of the world, to better understand how and why the roots to the Feminine were cut off and how its power was diminished.

During the last ice age the inland ice did not reach the ocean on the northern part of the Atlantic coast of present day Norway, due to the warmer waters of the Gulf Stream – a fact that has been confirmed by geological research. According to one theory groups of Sami, Finns, Basques, Celts and Norse people survived the ice age here. Similarities regarding words in their primitive languages, blood, scull shapes, ancient myths, boat types and many other things, show that there are connections between them. Traces of 10,000 to 13,000 year old settlements have also been found in this region.

These groups of people must have lived a harsh and isolated life in between the inland ice and the ocean. Conditions were most probably challenging, with incessant struggles against cold, wind and ice. Food was easily accessible though, since animal life was also concentrated to these ocean bays. The mountain caves, that sheltered them from ice as well as water, was seen as their steadfast, secure protector. This shield against the hardships of the outer world is believed to have created a specific concept, where a parallel reality of light, warmth and abundance of food was found in the inner parts of these mountains. Cliff is called *Hel* or *hellir* in ancient Nordic. The Norse Mother Goddess was also called Hel and was said to reside in the underworld. In the womb of Hel all wounds were healed.

Destructive Forces

In her revelatory book *The Chalice and the Blade*, Riane Eisler asks the question: "What is it that chronically tilts us toward cruelty rather than kindness, toward war rather than peace?" Her book suggests that neither war, nor inequality of gender, were part of our common roots. Backed up by extensive research she describes the transition from the Old European culture, that was based on partnership and peace, to one of domination. This development didn't just change civilization. It changed everything – how we relate to others, the way we look at nature, our basic beliefs about the universe as well as what, and how, we worship. It even changed how we perceive our identity, and thus our relationship to the clothes we wear.

A cataclysmic turning point of enormous magnitude changed the direction of the Old European cultures. The first signs might have been insignificant activities from nomadic bands, roaming the fringe areas of settlements while seeking grass for their herds. Over time they probably grew in numbers and ferocity. By the 5th millennium BC there is clear evidence of invasions, along with enormous destruction. In three concentrated waves, between 4,300 and 2,800 BC, the peaceful civilizations of Old Europe were subjected to physical and cultural disruption.

So who were these invaders? Marija Gimbutas refers to them as Kurgans, a nomadic culture from the Black Sea, the Caucasus and the Pontic-Caspian steppe, who swarmed into the European continent. (Even though Gimbutas' findings have been challenged by conventional archeologists, DNA studies support her theories.) Since their culture emphasized conquest and "Sky Gods" of war, it was totally different from that of Old Europe.

There were also other invaders, like the early Semites who invaded Canaan. The similarities and possible common origins of these two invading groups have been a question of debate, but in this context the interesting thing are the beliefs and values that unite them. Contrary to the peaceful cultures of Old Europe, these horse-riding tribes were a warring people, ruled by powerful priests and kings. They brought with them fierce and angry male gods of war and mountains. Their social and ideological systems were based on a model where the norm was male dominance and violence. Their structures were hierarchic, patriarchal and authoritarian.

> Patriarchy is a system
> that holds some men as superior to others
> and all men superior to women.
> *Carol Gilligan*

These tribes began to gradually impose their ideology and way of life on the peoples of the lands they conquered. The Mother Goddess, who was connected to Earth, was replaced by their Sky God. In accordance with their motto *Divide and Conquer*, her wholeness was split up into many, less potent, feminine archetypes. A male priest now became the authority, and sole interpreter, of "higher" spiritual realms. This was a way to gain power and keep the masses away from the old religion.

In this process the meaning of "dark" also changed from mysterious, magic and fertile into sinful and evil. People were led to believe that the "dark world below" was an evil place called hell that you could be sent to as punishment for not following Christian rules (note the obvious resemblance to the warm world below in the Goddess Hel*s caves, that were the steadfast protector that provided shelter for the survivors on the Norwegian coast during the last Ice Age).

Rituals like spiritual initiations were twisted into evil barbaric rites. In the myth *Ariadne's Thread* her labyrinth was inhabited by a scary monster who ate people, called the Minotaur (a bull was originally a sacred symbol and labyrinths were used for spiritual initiations). The one who kills this beast in this myth is, of course, a young Greek hero.

This distortion of spiritual practices, as well as the rewriting of myths, was a common way to ingrain new contexts as well as behaviors. Gradually the new patriarchal belief system took hold, in which a feminine spirituality, based on a close interaction with Nature and a direct relationship to the Divine (and therefore accessible to everyone), was no longer allowed to exist. The mindset that has dominated Western culture since then is that man stands apart from nature, above it and in control of it.

During this time of chaos a period of regression and stagnation set in, and cultural development seemed to come to a standstill. Two thousand years would elapse before Sumer, the so-called cradle of civilization, was at its height. Patriarchal values had now successfully replaced earlier values of equality and peace, while misogyny and hierarchal societies had become established. A different view of the origins and development of civilization, where Old Europe was seen as primitive, had also been accepted. The name Sumer actually means "land of the civilized kings" and their complex religion involved gods called the Anunnaki.

The Minoan Culture

A s the Old European cultures gradually lost their hold, one of them managed to preserve the system of equality for a long time, probably because it was situated on a distant island. This was the ancient civilization of Crete. Its story began around 6,000 BC when immigrants, who brought the Goddess and an agrarian technology with them, arrived at its shores. Some theories suggest that the gradual onset of invasions on the main land drove refugees to seek shelter on Crete. In safe isolation on this fertile island its cities developed and flourished for more than four thousand years.

This Minoan culture was first discovered at the turn of the 20th century and after decades of excavation archeologists were dumbfounded. They couldn't understand how the very existence of such a highly developed civilization could have remained unknown for so long. Their findings show a flourishing culture, where the high standard of living would have been seen as modern even today. No homes suggested poor living conditions. Urban centers had drainage systems, sanitary installations and domestic conveniences. There were viaducts, paved roads, reservoirs and large scale irrigation works. The Minoans were also skilled seafarers who traded goods with people around the Aegean Sea and far down in Egypt.

There seems to be a clear focus on living harmoniously and aesthetically, and the worship of nature pervaded everything. An enchanting and joyful artistic style evolved, that seemed to express the complete acceptance of the grace of life, so typical of Crete. Some called it the most inspired art in the ancient world. The high grade of refinement and architecture of its palaces is also unique. The great Palace of Knossos is famous for its "feminine spirit" of architecture. Its frescoes are painted in soft, flowing lines and there's a superb blend of life-enhancing and eye-pleasing features in vivid colors. Entertainment and spirituality were often intertwined, making Cretan leisure activities both pleasurable and meaningful. Their clothing was designed for both aesthetic effect and practicality, allowing freedom of movement.

The relationship between the sexes also appears to differ from what we are used to in our time. There seems to have been a frank appreciation of sexual differences and the pleasures made possible – a "pleasure bond" that would have strengthened a sense of mutuality between women and men as individuals.

Minoans were an exceptionally peace-loving people and ego-centered ambition seems non-existent, even among the ruling classes. There are no statues of those who sat on the thrones of Knossos or of any of the palaces, nor were records of the deeds of a ruler found. Nowhere was the name of an artist or author attached to a work of art. The idea of a warrior monarch triumphing in the humiliation and slaughter of the enemy is also absent. Their art show no grandiose scenes of battle or hunting, no idealization of violence nor any destructive use of power. There is a stark contrast to the monuments of authority and power that are so characteristic of Sumer, Egypt, Rome and other cultures that are based on domination.

Even if Crete might seem like a mythical paradise, it was a real human society. There were, of course, problems and imperfections and they did have weapons. As warfare and piracy increased in the Mediterranean they also fought sea battles to protect their shores and their vast maritime commerce. But warfare wasn't idealized, which makes a big difference.

The Minoan culture is the only known highly developed civilization where the worship of the Goddess survived into historical times. Around 2,000 BC, when the rest of "the civilized" world was steadily displacing her with warlike male gods, a Goddess still stands at the center in Crete.

Most of Crete's influence was lost around 1,400 BC, when the Palace of Knossos was destroyed. If this was due to volcanic eruptions and / or invasions of Dorians (a people from the north of Greece) is uncertain, but by 1,200 BC the Minoan culture collapsed. Even though remnants of the civilization survived, its cultural influence vanished.

The Demise of the Goddess

For thousands of years creation myths were passed down orally from generation to generation. Around the 9th to the 10th century, when the knowledge of writing in Roman letters reached the Nordic countries of Scandinavia, *The Völuspá* – Old Norse for "Prophecy of the Völva (a highly respected female seeress or shaman)"– was written down. It became the first and best known poem in *The Poetic Edda*, a collection of Old Norse narrative poems which is one of the most important primary sources for the study of Norse mythology.

> In the beginning there was Hel.
> Sea nor cool waves nor sand there were;
> Earth had not been, nor heaven above,
> But a yawning Ginnungagap, and grass nowhere.
> *The Völva*

The Völva begins by requesting silence and then directs her words to humankind and Odin, the one who had called upon her skills. Odin is a complex and multifaceted god who represents the wise All-father, but also the god of war. He has sacrificed one eye to be able to see everything that happens in the outside world (an interesting fact that ties in to the discussion in the chapter "Two Sides of a Whole").

The Völva goes on to describe that in the beginning there was only the Goddess Hel. Ginnungagap (everything that exists) was born from her womb. What she goes on to share doesn't portray an episode in the life of gods or people, nor is it cautionary as is common in the later Edda poems. It simply tells the story of the creation of the world and the first man and woman. She describes Yggdrasil, the central sacred tree of life, in which all worlds, that of humans as well as gods, nestle among its branches and roots. It represents the connection between all things, the life cycle, the cosmos, destiny, time and most importantly; harmony and balance between all things. Yggdrasil is closely related to the Tree of Life, a motif found across many cultures, and the Tree of Knowledge, which was said to grow in the Garden of Eden in Abrahamic religions. The Völva also talks about Ragnarök (the undoing of our civilization) and ends with a short, enchanted portrayal of the new and better world that will follow.

Around the 10th century Norse pagan beliefs began to be influenced by Christianity. There was a transitional period where they co-existed, so it took some time until Hel, the Norse Great Mother, fell into oblivion. When the tales of mythology were written down in *Eddan* she was still known, even though her power had been radically diminished. In the latter added parts of Eddan, written in the 12th to 13th century, Christian ideas are found through quotes like "the mighty one who rules over all". Paganism eventually gave way to Christianity, which was declared the official religion in Scandinavia. From some time onwards, Paganism was only tolerated if it was practiced in private.

Based on surviving texts The Goddess Hel was gradually banished. We eventually forgot that a Goddess had been at the center of our deepest beliefs. What stayed on was a name that *everybody* knows, now equivalent to the ultimate form of punishment and suffering – the concept of Hell, the terrifying world of fierce flames below, that we should all try to avoid by adhering to Christian beliefs, as well as practices.

Even though few Swedes are aware of the Norse Goddess Hel today, her name has been imprinted in our language through concepts like *hel* (whole, complete), *helig* (holy), *hela* (heal), *helhet* (entirety / wholeness), *helg* (holiday / holy day) and *helga* (to hallow / sanctify).

Image Versus Word

E very civilization, or larger settlement, needs some kind of writing as a way to store and pass on knowledge, and its origins are ancient. In 2012, as the Canadian paleoanthropologist and rock art researcher Genevieve von Petzinger analyzed ice age cave art created by humans between 10,000 to 40,000 years ago, she discovered that the same geometric signs have been used as a kind of alphabet by humans all over the world. The inherent meaning of basic shapes and symbols seems to be stored in our collective subconscious and trigger the recognition of a deeper content.

Using symbols to communicate is actually a very sophisticated form of communication. Without uttering a word these *ideograms* describe an entire concept that is not colored by beliefs or moral values. Since there is no forward or backward direction as in modern language, they belong to a more timeless and experiential realm.

The Vinča symbols (6,000-5,000 BC), found in present-day Serbia, are an evolution of these ideograms through modification by lines, curves and dots. This increased their complexity and culminated in *The Tărtăria Tablets*. It has been difficult to accurately date these, but some scientists suggest that they are from around 5,300 BC. While some archaeologists regard them as the earliest known form of linear script in the world, there is mounting evidence that this kind of script was a universal feature of the Old European civilizations.

There is some disagreement as to where the writing system we are used to today was invented. The first letters seem to have been created in Egypt to serve as an aid in writing Egyptian hieroglyphs. Sometime between 1,850 and 1,700 BC a group of Semitic-speaking people adopted some of these to represent the sounds of their language. This script is often considered the first alphabetic writing system, where unique symbols stood for single consonants, while vowels were omitted. Others claim that it was the Phoenicians that began to capture the different sounds of words through letters, and that their system is the ultimate ancestor of many modern scripts. Instead of having to remember hundreds or thousands of pictograms, only a couple of dozen letters were needed to represent any word.

An alphabet is a set of letters
written to represent particular sounds
in a spoken language.

By 800 BC this alphabet had spread to Greece, where it was refined and enhanced to record the Greek language. Some characters were kept and others were removed, while the real innovation was the use of new letters to represent vowels. Many scholars believe it was this addition, which made text more easily read and pronounced, that marked the creation of the first "true" alphabet. Over time it developed into the Latin alphabet that is now the most common writing system in use.

With the invention of a less complex alphabet that was a representation of sounds, it became possible for ordinary women and men to learn how to read and write. It helped capture, express and pass on a full range of thoughts and ideas. A more detailed way of recording facts and historical events was also made possible. Whether these texts were reliable or not depended on the perspective, and bias, of the person who wrote it, though.

So why is this important? The transition from symbols to an alphabet that imitates spoken sounds and words signifies a monumental shift in our evolution. Since the cognitive processes involved are worlds apart, the circuits of our human brains were rewired. Just like a work of art that provides an experience for the observer, or dreams that are vivid in our memory but impossible to adequately describe in words, the symbols and ideograms that were originally used to communicate speak directly to subconscious levels. They bypass rational thinking and are directly transferred to the right side of the brain, where there is a recognition of its holistic content and deeper meaning. This provides a direct experience beyond words and rationality.

Alphabetic writing and reading, on the other hand, helped us evolve abstract thinking, the ability to reflect on our own thoughts and gain a spectator's perspective. But letters of the alphabet use the logical-rational cognition of the left-brain that splits time, space and qualities into polarities. When we form words they might (depending on the interaction between the two brain lobes of the individual that is reading them) spark an association to their deeper meaning. But it focuses our cognitive functions on a more shallow level. Even though words have a clear and specific rational meaning, many have a positive or negative connotation that is often charged with opinions, cultural biases and preconceived ideas, specific to the person.

> The structure of a language shapes or limits our worldview
> and thus determines how we perceive and experience everything.
> *The Sapir-Whorf Hypothesis*

The development of the alphabet thus focused our cognitive processes to the left side of our brains. In his book *The Alphabet Versus the Goddess - The Conflict Between Word and Image*, Leonard Shlain calls it "the dark side of literacy". He claims that this development was what brought on the demise of the Goddess worshipping civilizations of Old Europe, initiated the decline of the feminine and ushered in the reign of patriarchy and misogyny. It shifted our intuitive, holistic, right-brain orientation, expressed through images and symbols, to one that is more linear, fragmented and left-brain centered. Thus the rise of alphabetic literacy fundamentally reconfigured our human brains, which brought profound changes to the development of civilization.

Two Sides of a Whole

T here is an inner duality embedded in the psyche of women and men alike. Due to the development of a deep cultural imbalance, along with the kind of languages we use to read and write, we tend to approach these poles as if there was a conflict of interest. A semi-conscious value system lies behind this collective conditioning, where one pole is favored while the other is considered inferior. Regardless of whether this imbalance is experienced on a personal level, or through our cultural Story and the systems and institutions that have been born out of it, the result is always the same: It leads to polarity and conflict. Since this state of consciousness has so many negative consequences, our most crucial challenge is to restore this balance.

Since we are used to regarding some of the differences as gender-related, the poles are often referred to as *feminine* and *masculine*. But it is not as simple as men or women being, or behaving, in certain ways. Generally speaking the feminine is not exclusive to women, nor do masculine qualities belong to men. That said, there are intricate hormonal processes that influence our behaviors.

The human psyche is complex, which makes it important to raise this discussion beyond gender. A better metaphor to describe these poles, and remove them from the Western value system, is through the concept of *Yin and Yang*. In Chinese philosophy these are complementary forces in a dynamic, interconnected and interdependent system that forms a greater whole. One gives rise to the other and inherent in each of them is a tiny part of its opposite. Yin represents the hidden instinctive, intuitive and semiconscious worlds, along with the primal, cyclical aspects of nature. It is inclusive and seeks coopera-  tion. Yang is focused awareness. It deals with what is manifested – the imposition of structure over chaos and thus pursuits reason, ideals and universal truths. Yang energy separates and tends to compete. While yin is dark, cold, moist and passive, yang is light, warm, dry and active. Their relationship is one of simultaneous attraction and repulsion, which is what creates energy, movement and life.

Our brain is a polarity organ that mirrors these complimentary parts. Its two hemispheres represent different ways to understand and relate to life. We can also see them as distinct forms of awareness. It is important to note that the essence of who we are lies beyond this polarity. Consciousness is not equal to the brain. This is seen through many studies of near-death experiences with vivid memories under circumstances when brain functions are completely disabled. But let's take a closer look at what makes the poles different.

Yin and the right brain
DIFFUSE AWARENESS - BEING - EXPERIENCE - CONTENT - INNER KNOWING/WISDOM
The non-verbal side of the brain develops first in the embryo. It is an awareness with blurred boundaries. In this state everything becomes alive – continuously morphing, expanding and contracting. As in chaos theory there are no predictable patterns, nor linear processes.

This Yin part of us helps us be still, rest, reflect and conserve. This puts us in tune with our emotions and gut feelings. Highly intuitive it helps us instantly recognize what facial expressions, gestures and body language mean, which helps us discern people's character and intent. It is also sensitive to energies and can register the prevailing mood in any location. Along with these abilities it is easy to grasp the deeper meaning behind colors, shapes and symbols. Music, dance and art are typical right-brain activities that allow us to express ourselves freely, without any necessity to try to squeeze our experiences into limiting words.

There is also spacial and field awareness that helps us zoom out to relate to several layers or perspectives of an issue. We can thus grasp a deeper meaning behind things, as well as complex interrelationships and processes, which would be impossible to see, or even be open to, from a purely logical perspective. In this kind of awareness we are not even limited by time and space. It is a portal to invisible worlds, hidden messages and altered states of consciousness, where mystery rules over logic, and where conventional rules of reasoning are defied. Since this way of relating to life connects us to our essence and inner knowing, the Soul and Spirit become our true authority.

Without a balanced connection to the focused discernment and structure of Yang awareness and the left brain, there can be a tendency to believe in everything "mysterious". Life can become truly chaotic.

Yang and the left brain
FOCUSED AWARENESS - DOING - INTENT - FORM - KNOWLEDGE
We find our center for speech, writing and abstract thinking in the left brain. This part of us is rational and structured, and has a superb ability for discernment. It can focus on details, analyze and sort things into objects and categories. In this process things, as well as traits, are separated from each other, which makes it possible to categorize, prioritize and organize. Without this kind of awareness we wouldn't even be able to exist in our 3-dimensional world, nor be oriented in time and space.

When Yang awareness and the left-brain is favored there is focus on outer form. We look for answers in the external world, tend to live according to contemporary ideals and listen to the appointed authorities in different fields. Clear decisions are made and action is taken. Our lives are well planned and managed. We are well aware of scientific, financial and historical facts. The human body is seen from a more material point of view, consisting of mechanics, electricity and chemistry.

But knowing the name of a tree, for instance, can become more important than actually experiencing it. If we are over-reliant on Yang qualities and the left brain, what isn't palpable and rational doesn't exist at all. Things related to inner experiences and spirituality are seen as mere fantasy, wishful thinking or woo woo. There is little or no contact with feelings, our soul and deeper experiences.

> The intuitive mind is a sacred gift
> and the rational mind its faithful servant.
> We have created a society that
> honors the servant and has forgotten the gift.
> *Albert Einstein*

Even though there is always some kind of interaction between these two poles in a functioning individual, one tends to dominate. And when one side is idealized (regardless of what that part is) a problem occurs, because its opposite is automatically devalued. We end up with conflict and strife. Without a natural interaction with its opposite, the part that is overvalued also turns into something negative.

These polarized ways of perceiving life have different inherent values. Since the left-brain is emphasized in school, and is often seen as superior in Western culture, this is what most people tend to lean towards. It restricts our life experience. A world where yin qualities are seen with a negative bias is a world full of competition, exclusion and war, violence against women and abuse of animals and nature. In the patriarchal value system that stems from this imbalance, the feminine is regarded as a weaker, inferior part. The feminine ideal in this narrow perspective includes qualities like being soft, nurturing, submissive and adaptable, even though true yin qualities are so much more complex and have such strength and depth. Women have carried this stigma for thousands of years, and have become scapegoats for skewed feminine qualities.

As most already know, this is an outdated way of looking at this polarity, as well as gender roles. No power struggles between them is necessary. The interaction needed between these counterparts can best be understood through the metaphor of a tree. The roots and the crown depend on each other, and none would exist without the other. Both types of awareness' are totally necessary to our lives. Getting there requires a stretch though, which involves inner development.

A great mind is androgynous.
When the two sides of the brain are balanced and integrated
a mutual fertilization takes place
which creates an extraordinary phenomenon.
Samuel Coleridge

From Wholeness to Separation

T he cultural shift from partnership to domination, and the development of written language from symbols to an alphabet, changed our perception of the world in similar ways. They also occurred in the same timespan, which is intriguing. Did one lead to the other, or were they simply two different aspects of an evolutionary cycle?

Even though it's impossible to know for sure how our prehistoric ancestors perceived the world as well as themselves before this shift, it seems obvious that their experience of life was more whole, without a clear separation between what is now divided into inner and outer, or feminine and masculine. Most probably they had a more symbiotic relationship to each other as well as nature, which would have involved interaction with the elemental and energetic forces on our planet. The cultural shift towards separation and competition must have felt like leaving the Garden of Eden. It is also weirdly similar to "eating an apple from the Tree of Knowledge", which could be seen as a metaphor for beginning to favor left-brain qualities. Over time this changed the structure of our human identity. As the left-brain began to dominate, a self-model of duality made us lose our connection to source and a deeper understanding of life. Since an unaware Ego feeds on separation and duality, it must have gained a whole new position in our psyche.

What we perceive has to be interpreted and organized by the brain, otherwise it would remain meaningless and make no sense to us. So a model of the world is required. This belief system predisposes us to interpret reality in a specific way, make conclusions, make sense of our experiences and gather evidence of their validity. We agree on how to do things as well as the rules behind all practices and disciplines (like our way of relating to clothes). The prevailing Story also determines which experiences we collectively accept as "real" and which we reject as "illusion". What we call reality is thus based on the existing paradigm, which makes it extremely powerful.

A civilization built on partnership and one based on domination are two totally contrasting principles of organization, two alternative structures that affect our cultural, social as well as technological evolution. The dominator culture thus led to a specific paradigm where reality was split into parts. This hierarchal and authoritarian system began to shape every cultural arena. In our culture we are thus trained, from an early age, to not experience reality holistically.

The strategy *Divide and Conquer* describes how power is gained and maintained in this kind of system. Since parts that are split-off from the whole have less power, division is created. Smaller groups are prevented from linking up by fostering distrust and enmity between individuals, while those who are willing to cooperate with the sovereign are supported and promoted.

This strategy is used in many different fields. It somehow resembles the world of fashion too. Since ideals are something we look up to, and strive towards, beauty ideals invoke a subtle form of competition. All the different trends and clothing styles are really just split-off fragments of attitudes and behaviors. In modern western culture we can choose to identify with any of the clothing styles, which is great on one hand. But identifying with parts that are split off from the whole is also one of our collective dilemmas. Since none of the parts can embody the whole, we cannot access the power of an integrated psyche.

CULTURE AS A SHAPING MOLD
Ideals of Beauty

We see them everywhere – in images that flood all kinds of media, mannequins in clothing stores and fashion models on the catwalk – the perfect woman, our ideal of a man. Both are put on a pedestal as some kind of goal to aspire to. They look nothing like most of us. But on some deeper level we keep comparing ourselves to these cultural fantasies of what a man and a woman should look like. What we should be like.

People who embody a timeless beauty to their physical form definitely exist. Let's continue to revel in it. But this is only one layer of beauty. All of us have a unique inner Beauty, a specific blend of deeper characteristics, that can be given an outer expression.

On a cultural level there are vast variations to what we see as beautiful, but this collective opinion is more shallow. It also shifts and changes. Without a healthy connection to Self we are prone to be influenced by these ideals. We begin to identify with how we are seen in the eyes of others. Depending on whether we can live up to cultural ideals or not, we either feel good or bad about ourselves. Beauty is thus like a double-edged sword. One kind is related to Self love, the other to Self denial.

In a culture that focuses on externals
inauthenticity is deep. It is even rewarded.
Gabor Maté

The prevailing beauty standards in Western culture has dominated fashion, art and design for several thousand years. They are based on ideals that developed in old Greece, a civilization that put a lot of emphasis on the research and discovery of the ideal human appearance. The earliest theories about beauty originated in pre-socratic Greek philosophy. Followers of Pythagoras believed that there was a strong connection between mathematics and beauty. An object with proportions in accordance with the golden section was experienced as more attractive, which led to an ideal of symmetry and proportion. These beauty ideals were considered immortal and unchangeable. Despite the truth and importance of these harmonic proportions it also had negative consequences. One result was ideas about the "perfect" human body, where irregularities were not permitted.

This aesthetic mindset also connected beauty to morality and good-ness. A person with a beautiful appearance was seen as someone who had positive personal traits and thus higher value. This is why heroes, gods and goddesses in Greek mythology were portrayed as being so perfect in their beauty. Men were exhibited naked, young and thin, with defined muscles, blue eyes and golden blonde hair. The female body was represented by soft shapes, full breasts, round buttocks, long legs, long hair with golden curls and a gentle face. Both sexes had flawless proportions and incomparable perfection.

Since man was raised to a level of "divine perfection", the beauty ideals of ancient Greece were quite unreal and impossible to live up to. This was further enhanced by raising sculptures of perfect looking gods and goddesses on pedestals. Even though a pedestal is simply the name we have given to a piece of furniture that functions as a base, the saying "putting someone on a pedestal" describes our habit of raising someone in esteem and value. We look up to them as an ideal to aspire to. Which, obviously, is one of the drivers behind fashion.

Christianity further reinforced this split between "good and bad" through emphasizing concepts like good vs evil, light vs darkness and right vs wrong. What evolved was a pattern of either valuing or devaluing. In a belief system where some traits or personal expressions are raised and idealized, their counterparts are automatically looked down upon. So we strive to identify with the good and avoid the bad.

This Greek perception of beauty still has a strong hold on Western culture. A slim and muscular man with a vigorous physique is considered virile and attractive. For a woman the beauty standard often involves our lips, breasts, waistline and buttocks. The only thing that changes is what part of the body is in focus, as well as its size. The rounded, soft shapes of antiquity has now been replaced by a smaller size with more defined muscles. More like a man.

> There is no exquisite beauty
> without some strangeness in the proportion.
> *Edgar Allan Poe*

Is beauty really something that can be evaluated rationally, or calculated through mathematical laws? What about that quirky irregular nose that makes the expression of a person absolutely irresistible, or the surprising mix between a perfect musical chord and a dissonance? Isn't that what makes humans, art as well as life, intriguing?

The truth is that perfect doesn't really exist. Sure, there is a certain symmetry and proportion to our bodies, but imperfection is what makes us human. In her book *Addiction to Perfection* the Jungian analyst Marion Woodman looks at how this pursuit of perfection, due to a polarized belief system that splits things into good and bad, is inhibiting our development. Trapped in this dilemma we might become highly respected professionals with a perfect facade, but the communication between the mask and the inner being will often be missing. This might lead to a feeling of emptiness that can result in compulsive behaviors like eating disorders or overconsumption.

Not all cultures have beauty ideals that are based on perfection. An inspiring example is the traditional Japanese aesthetic ideal called *Wabi Sabi – the art of impermanence*, that still lingers in modern Japan. With roots in Zen buddhism it promotes a different approach to beauty, as well as to life. Two simple realities are acknowledged: Nothing is perfect. Everything is transient.

The Wabi Sabi approach to beauty is inspired by nature, where everything is interconnected and co-exists in harmony. Sun and rain, budding and withering exist side by side, like two sides of the same coin. You cannot separate one from the other and none has more value than the other. They are merely different phases of the natural process of time – an expression of the circular flow of nature in a universe in constant change and evolution. In order to perceive innate beauty we are encouraged to look beyond the mere physical form.

In Western culture women are usually seen as less attractive as they grow older, which has resulted in an obsession to try to turn back the clock through make-up, hair dye, different fillers and plastic surgery. We can become stuck in the illusion that we lose something with age and don't want to be part of these natural cycles. The Wabi Sabi ideal looks at this differently. It honors the interplay between youth and old age, life and death, because it is the rhythm of Nature. The highest form of beauty can only be attained with time, which means that age is revered instead of seen as a disadvantage. Wrinkles and grey hair are a true sign of this transient beauty. A beautiful woman is the one who is natural and genuine, since our true beauty – our essence – is revealed as time peals off the outer layers.

> That which is absolutely still or absolutely perfect is absolutely dead
> for without the possibility of growth and change
> there can be no Tao.
> *Taoist philosophy*

From this perspective of beauty, design is better defined by what is left out than by what is put in. Even though there is attention to detail, the key is to try to keep all design aspects simple. Wabi Sabi beauty can be a worn jacket, free of details, in a handcrafted, creased linen with irregularities and imperfections. The natural wear and tear of the textile materials is seen as adding to the beauty through the changes of texture and color. The Western perspective of beauty, on the other hand, tends to make us add details and use inorganic materials to strive for unnatural perfection and thus defy the aging processes.

The Japanese plain running stitch technique called Sashiko was first applied to clothing out of a practical need and was used to mend tears as well as to reinforce clothing around points of wear. Worn out clothes were also pieced together to make new garments by using this simple type of embroidery. On top of making the clothes more durable, each layer of patches and embroidery added beauty to the garments. Sashiko has now become an art form. Needless to say, this could only unfold in a culture where natural resources are valued.

The difference between grandeur and simplicity, as well as symmetry and asymmetry, is another obvious difference in these two ways of looking at beauty. Unlike Western Hellenic-inspired ideals of beauty, where cities have squares, avenues, colonnades and cathedrals that are usually constructed with precise symmetry, Wabi Sabi has nothing to do with grandeur, nor symmetry. It is more of an understated beauty that exists in the modest, rustic, imperfect or even in the decayed. Beauty is something hidden that we need to make an effort to search for through stripping off outer layers. This is how essence is revealed. The same differences can be observed if we compare an impressive European garden design to the subtle beauty of a Japanese garden, with its careful arrangement of stones, water and trees. The observer is not invited to be impressed by grandeur, but is enticed to simply contemplate and take in the calm, harmonious atmosphere.

The connection between these two very different beauty ideals to the polarity of yin and yang, as well as the values of the right and left brain, seems quite obvious. The specific development of Western culture led us to abandon ideas that there is a deeper reality behind form. We closed the door to a more holistic view of life and began to limit ourselves to beliefs that are rather narrow. Hopefully we have reached a point in time where we are free to reject outdated ideals as well as the myth of flawless beauty.

PART II

Dressed for Growth

We are built to grow. We are destined to grow.
A caterpillar is not supposed to die as a caterpillar.
Its destiny is to grow wings and fly.
Robert Kegan

As we return from this deep dive into the development of civilizations, languages and beauty ideals, a few things have become obvious: The result of the cultural shifts led to certain imbalances and skewed perspectives that changed the state of human consciousness. It led to the specific mindsets that created the Old Story. This formed the foundation that Western culture rests upon and that our societal systems, as well as different industries, are built on.

So how do we find our way forward? The first step is to question outdated beliefs and ideals. The next is to acknowledge that the development of a culture depends upon the inner growth of its inhabitants. The same goes for an industry and its customers. This part of the book is thus focused on inner development. We will take a closer look at what design is really about, as well as the different parts of our human identity. Some specific stages of growth, that are accompanied by the emergence of new needs and inner drives, will be explored. Each stage also changes our relationship to clothes. They can even help us along in these inner processes.

The Essence of Clothing Design

Fashion is about constant change. But has this led to anything more progressive than a shift of styles? One result is a more relaxed relationship to earlier, very strict dress codes, along with more freedom to express ourselves the way we want. The basic concept of clothing remains the same though: Garments cover and protect our bodies, provide practical functions and signify social code. I believe it is time to expand this concept. In search for ways to develop the way we relate to, and use clothes, we need to begin by looking at what clothing design is really about.

Clothes communicate in their own specific ways. But what makes their language different from other creative expressions? Contemporary issues are often explored through art, but this is rarely the case with clothes. Different combinations of garments, and the way they are worn, speak more about attitudes, traits and qualities. Like architecture they are a form of applied art, although not stationary like buildings. In their movement, color combinations and repetitive visual patterns they are more similar to music, even though they don't fade out as tones do. Clothes can be part of the expression in other arts. In theater and film a character emerges as the actor dresses in the costume that helps her or him embody, as well as portray, a specific kind of person with a certain mix of traits. In dance they amplify the overall mood and symbolism of the story. Even though clothes can definitely be an art form in themselves, our everyday clothes have very little meaning without a body and a cultural setting. Since the garments we wear are also a personal choice, and something we identify with, the wearer is key.

We all wear clothes. But we wear them, and need them, for different reasons. The most apparent of the needs they fill is that they protect us. They are also practical. But even though these aspects are definitely important reasons for wearing them, clothes also help us fill other needs. Looking back in history it is obvious that different dress codes and fashions have had the purpose of somehow changing the person wearing them. Showing status, authority or profession. Hinting at certain characteristics, specific attitudes as well as conveying subtle messages about modesty, sensuality, or trustworthiness.

What is design then? Many would answer that it's about the colors and shapes of a product — the unique style of a dress or the interesting fabric pattern of a shirt. But even though this is what we usually refer to when we talk about design, it is much more than what meets the eye. Design, as opposed to art, is always about serving the user with specific functions. At its core, design is about creating something that offers *a solution to different needs*. If you design a cup, for instance, it satisfies our need to contain the liquid as well as to ingest it. It also needs to be easy to lift it and fit comfortably into our hand. A towel meets our need to remove water, or other liquids, from our hands or body. The more efficient and pleasant these things are, the more we appreciate them.

Good design is always a balance between form and function, so aesthetics is not a top priority. The function of a garment is based on experience, so to better understand the needs a product is made to fill reality has to be examined. When you design a chair you explore how well different shapes and materials satisfy the need to sit comfortably, accommodate our body and support our back. When clothes are designed we test how much movement a garment allows, if its practical functions work as intended and if the material feels nice to the skin. We might also experiment with how much to show or hide of a specific body part. With clothes there is also the need to feel good with their style, colors and patterns.

When I left my job as an employed designer, with the quest of finding a deeper and more meaningful way to work with clothes, I was confused about my professional role. If I had chosen a different design field, like furniture or kitchen utensils, the function of the objects, and what they were needed for, would have been clear. But when your design field is clothes and fabric patterns for clothes, what you work with is so closely tied to the human identity and the culture we live in.

It was obvious to me that I needed to explore the connection between the clothes we wear and our identity. I needed to take a closer look at which attitudes, traits and qualities were strengthened by different styles, shapes and color combinations. But without more knowledge about the psychology and evolution of a human being, along with a deeper understanding of the development of our culture, this would not be possible. It was as puzzling as intriguing to me that this was not a self-evident part of every design education. It was as if we had forgotten something essential.

A Closer Look at Identity

A s I embarked on this path of exploration I knew, deep down, that figuring out what inner growth was really about meant that I had to begin with myself. The only things we know for sure are those we have experienced.

With this in mind I began to explore my own psyche. How had I become the person I was? What forces ruled my behavior along with my choice of clothes? As mentioned earlier I turned to psychoanalysis, shadow work, art therapy, meditation and many other methods. One of these turned out to be really important in my understanding of identity. *Voice Dialogue, the psychology of selves*, is a way to raise self-awareness and transform consciousness through dialogue with different inner parts, or energy patterns, in our psyche. Hal and Sidra Stone, who developed the method, are both clinical psychologists and have written several books about it.

My experience with this process was nothing less than mind-blowing. As I tuned in to specific parts my body language and way of speaking totally changed. It all felt so natural and it was easy to experience their different energies. Some were childlike. Others were people pleasers or seemed old and wise beyond my comprehension. It became obvious that some character traits had developed as coping strategies to protect me in different ways. As we went deeper I was shocked to discover the viciousness of parts that had been denied and fascinated by what happened as I began to look beyond their nasty surface, understand and appreciate them. They were like hidden gems with priceless qualities.

Along with this inner exploration I took a deep intellectual dive into different frameworks that tried to explain the forces that shape what we perceive as identity. I delved into studies of humanistic and trans-personal psychology (which focuses on adult growth rather than mental illness), mythology, philosophy, religion, esoteric teachings and different traditions of human development. Some of these made more sense to me since they confirmed my own experiences.

Identity is often described as consisting of definite parts that appear in various situations. But an identity is actually a constant process of change where our genetics, culture, loved ones, those we care for, people who have harmed us and people we have harmed, good and bad things we've done, experiences lived and choices made, all influence us to become who we are at this particular moment. A human identity relates to different energetic patterns that are always in fluctuation and have no definite borders (they are more like circles that overlap at times). Since energy cannot be fully described in a logical, linear language, we need our right-brain to intuit their qualities. The words to describe different parts of the human identity also vary, which can lead to confusion. What do we really mean when we say psyche or personality?

Roberto Assagioli, a psychiatrist and a pioneer in the fields of humanistic and transpersonal psychology, founded the movement known as psychosynthesis. His *Egg Diagram* illustrates the multi-dimensional nature of the human psyche and how the various parts of one's consciousness relate to each other.

1 - Lower Unconscious

2 - Middle Unconscious / Here called Subconscious

3 - Higher Unconscious or Superconscious

4 - Field of Conscious Awareness

5 - The Conscious I / Here called The Personality (Ego, Persona)

6 - The Higher Self / Here called Self, Soul or Essence

7 - The Collective Unconscious

Below is a description of my own understanding of human consciousness. Knowing what I refer to makes it easier when I use these words in later chapters.

SPIRIT

For a long time I was confused about the difference between Spirit and Soul. Eventually I came to understand it like this: There is only one Spirit – the Source that we are all a part of. Some refer to it as God or the Universe. It exists outside of time and space, but manifests in different dimensions through the individual sparks that we refer to as our souls.

SOUL, ESSENCE or SELF

We all have a unique soul and are born with a core identity, also referred to as our higher or inner Self, or our Essence. Our Soul is a quiet center of awareness and is, at the same time, a synthesis of all our experiences. It contains certain deeper characteristics and a unique mix of talents. At the beginning of our lives we *are* that essence, but it is impossible for us to express it without the development of a personality and an ego. But in the process of conditioning, and the splitting into conscious and unconscious parts of us, this innate Self or Soul becomes (partly) hidden. If we have adults around us who can sense who we truly are, the connection can be supported.

This formless essence can be experienced through meditation and other mind-altering methods, but depends on the different facets of our

91

personality for expression. As we develop, and learn to balance the personality, our essence can become more present in our lives, along with its deeper qualities and unique talents.

THE PERSONALITY

As an open, trusting and impressionable child we are constantly fed with information. What begins as a description of the world, told from our caretakers perspective of life, becomes our reality. We haven't yet developed discernment and easily become trapped in narrow ways of looking at "reality". What lies beyond the world described to us becomes non-existent or turns into something mystical.

As we grow up some behaviors are rewarded while others are not appreciated. We might grasp this simply by sensing the atmosphere in our homes. It can also be very obvious, to the point where we are ridiculed or punished unless we behave in certain ways. What we call the personality is the set of traits, attitudes, thinking and behavior patterns, as well as relationship dynamics, that we are shaped by and begin to relate to as "who we are". A person could be identified by being thrifty, ambitious and intellectual, while the polar opposites – a generous side, a contentment with what is and a strong connection to emotions – become denied and are hidden on subconscious levels. Some might also revolt against who they are "supposed to be" and take on these opposite values. In the process of picking sides our inner balance, our wholeness, along with the connection to our Soul, is more or less lost.

Our personality is thus the primary inner parts that we identify with. Personal growth depends on our willingness to consciously expand and balance it.

THE PSYCHE consists of several layers:

Conscious

The conscious mind contains the thoughts, feelings, cognitions and memories we are aware of. But our conscious mind is only in control of small parts of what drives us. Around 95% of our automatic actions and reactions stem from levels beyond what we are conscious of.

Subconscious

Thoughts, feelings and memories that hover below our threshold of awareness belong to the subconscious. Information is registered and remembered here without any intention or effort. Things like riding a bike, swimming or tying our shoes become automatic. The subconscious influences our behavior, which makes us react and respond according to how we have been programmed.

As seen in the description of the personality, some behaviors were denied or disowned since they were not appreciated or accepted as we grew up. These are stored on subconscious levels. Emotional issues that have not been processed, along with unresolved trauma, can be experienced as anxiety, stress, difficulties to concentrate or a persistent irritable mood without any plausible explanation. Someone yelling at us, or treating us in a certain way, might trigger subconscious memories and evoke a strong automatic reactions.

There are a myriad of ways to process these hidden memories. By activating their content through different therapies, dream work, art or physical movement, a natural flow of energy can be reinstated. We can also reprogram our subconscious mind through meditation, visualization or hypnosis.

There are many ways to move past the thin barrier between conscious and subconscious levels. It dissolves in various degrees when we make inner journeys, dream, express ourselves through art, meditate or take drugs. Along with inner growth we can more easily access our psyche. This does not mean that we can make the subconscious conscious, but that we can become more aware of it and begin to build a deeper personal relationship to dream images, archetypes and symbols. The subconscious is an enormous resource in any creative pursuit, problem solving or inner guidance.

Unconscious

The unconscious is defined by a state where we are totally unaware of things around us. It consists of the deepest recesses of our past and hidden memories – traits that are so totally disowned and split of from our consciousness that they have become twisted into a demonic quality, experiences so terrifying that they needed to be repressed because we were not able to handle them, memories so traumatic that we just had to hide and forget about them. Unprocessed, and barred from consciousness, these are stuck in our bodies as tensions and blockages, and continue to influence our life experience as well as behaviors.

The way I understand it, the difference between subconscious and unconscious is related to the severity of the fear, anxiety, shame or guilt that are connected to different memories or traumas. I know from personal experience how scary it can be when repressed traumas surface. I was sexually abused when I was five, which was so terrifying that it was totally blocked. Through art therapy, dreams and hypnosis over a long period of time that began in my 30's, the memories started to rise to the surface. Even though some things were confirmed by my mom I continued to question if this had really happened to me or if I had some-how made it up. It was so deeply confusing to not have any conscious remembrance.

Many years later a terrifying and intriguing witchlike part of me emerged through the method called Voice Dialogue. She was the result of having disowned my personal power to such a degree that it had been twisted into a demonic character. Again there was this extreme confusion when I tried to grasp how this could be a part of my own psyche.

Superconscious

There is also a "higher" unconscious state. This is the source of our inspiration and higher intuition, as well as altruistic love and urges to humanitarian action. We reach this state through contemplation and meditation and might experience states of illumination and ecstasy.

Collective unconscious

Our individual psyche is not isolated but connected to the collective unconscious, which is made up of common human knowledge and paradigms, along with archetypes and shapes. We also share experiences of an ancient hidden past, ancestral experiences as well as deep human wounds and global traumas, that still influence us and lead to unresolved conflicts and wars.

On our path of inner growth the boundaries between these different states of consciousness begin to blur and become more transparent. Deep insights and symbols from dreams start to permeate our waking lives. We experience synchronicities and more subtle layers of reality. Beginning to access these more fluid and expansive states of consciousness signifies the awakening of non-dual consciousness.

This new awareness can lead to profound realizations about our own personal lives as well as the illusions of life in a larger sense. It can be exhilarating, but also quite confusing as to what is "real". During this process it is extra important to balance our inner life with the outer to maintain our grounding.

THE SHADOW

A strong tension is created when we are faced with an internal conflict. Our psyche deals with it by rejecting a part of us. The severity of the conflict determines if it is stored on a subconscious or unconscious level. We usually experience a loss of energy, while the subconscious becomes overcharged, resulting in emotional turmoil, inner stress or illness.

The parts of ourselves that are rejected and denied, because we perceive them as bad, become part of our Shadow. Depending on our conditioning these parts can become repressed, twisted and sometimes even demonized. They also turn into hidden inner drives.

We tend to project the characteristics of our Shadow to somebody else. In this way we can relate to them while we avoid accepting them. When we meet somebody who expresses a behavior that we refuse to acknowledge in ourselves, it usually throws us into negative feelings that can range from disapproval to anger or fear. This is a root cause for drama and conflicts in our lives. Every time we have a negative emotional reaction to somebody else's characteristics or behavior patterns, it is usually because of a trait we have disowned. We can choose to see this as a wake-up call, where we are shown what we need to embrace to become more whole.

Becoming aware of who we judge, and what specific qualities or behaviors tend to upset us (or at times even evoke admiration or infatuation) is a great way to get an insight into our shadow. Since energy cannot disappear the traits we disown won't go away, they can only be transformed. As we focus on this process we realize that the denied traits actually have a positive side that we can benefit from.

THE EGO

Our Ego is often seen as something negative. Some even say that we need to get rid of it. The reason for this bad reputation is that, in its unaware state, it is built upon a set of primary personality parts with specific coping mechanisms. These were developed to deal with challenging situations we experienced growing up. Our Ego's initial focus was to protect our vulnerability and thus avoid pain. Since it was first created out of fear, it can be controlling and driven by selfish needs.

But we need the Ego. We could not be grounded in our identity and this 3D reality without it. It holds a sort of executive function in our psyche, a focused decision-making part that we depend upon in everyday life. It is in contact with the external world and serves as the integrator of our outer and inner experiences. It determines what we show, what we share and which behaviors are adequate in a specific situation. So there is no need to obliterate it.

Since it tends to interpret and react to things out of early defense mechanisms, that might no longer be relevant, we *do* need to become aware of which primary parts of us are ruling it. As the process of examining our constricting attitudes and belief systems begins, our Ego opens up to include a larger variety of inner parts. Our Ego thus evolves into an *Aware Ego*. With this widening arena of perspectives and traits it can begin to make more informed choices.

> We are like books.
> Most people only see our cover.
> The minority only read the introduction
> and many people believe the critics.
> Few will know our content.
> *Emile Zola*

THE PERSONA

At the outer edge – the part of us that meets the external world – we find our Persona. This is our social mask, our chosen self-image and the parts we chose to exhibit when we interact with others. It is governed by the Ego and initially functions as a kind of armor that covers our vulnerability. But, just as any armor, it eventually becomes heavy and stops us from growing.

Our persona can be directly translated to clothes – at least the way they are normally used in Western culture. The garments we wear send out signals about which societal group(s) we belong to and the dress codes we have adopted to fit in on different occasions. We all have an everyday persona which consists of the traits we are most at ease with as we interact with the outer world. But our Persona depends on the setting.

In certain situations we need a different mask, for instance to show a stricter version of ourselves in a professional setting, to have more casual interactions in a social situation, or having fun playing. The closer we are to the people we interact with, the less is our need for a mask.

As our identity develops, we start to see through these social masks. Our core essence begins to permeate our identity and we become more genuine and authentic. In this process the Persona becomes more transparent. We begin to dress in clothes that are more in tune with the deeper characteristics of our core identity.

Before we look at how our relationship to the garments we wear changes along with human growth, let's just briefly compare the concepts of Personality, Ego, Persona and Self to clothes, since they are such great metaphors, as well as expressions, of different parts of our identity.

We can compare the PERSONALITY to our entire wardrobe. The garments we find there are usually a pretty good representation of the different parts of ourselves that we are aware of and identify with. Some might still end up in the back unused, which might give us hints about parts of ourselves we long to bring out in the open but that we, for some reason, are not entirely comfortable with. They might also represent parts that we are tired of, or bored with.

At the beginning of or journey of inner growth our EGO is expressed through the garments in the wardrobe we feel most safe and least vulnerable in. Maybe we feel most comfortable in black or beige, hesitant to show more colors. For some it can be the other way around.

The different outfits form our PERSONA. As mentioned earlier we have different personas, depending on the social situation. We might have a professional persona, or outfit, that suits different work occasions. There can also be specific clothes to wear to parties or dates, as well as some for outdoors activities.

At the beginning of our developmental path there is usually no sign of any SOUL or SELF in our wardrobe. Many women I have met and worked with describe a deep longing for a different type of clothes. You might have some idea of a kind of garment that is a bit blurry, or outfits you absolutely love but can't see yourself wearing since they don't fit into your ordinary life and culture. It might even feel scary to dress like that.

I certainly had that experience when I was young. What I longed for was a type of garment that didn't even fit into the time, nor the place, where I lived. Later on I made these garments for myself, but initially only wore them at home since it felt totally out of place to use them on ordinary occasions. As time went by though, they began to fit into my life, most of all as a result of becoming more comfortable with my core identity.

The Wisdom of the Pyramid

I n every time and culture we have looked for ways to help us understand life and the deeper underlying reality. On my own explorative journey I delved into esoteric teachings and different creation stories to try to grasp a bigger picture behind the formative forces that shape life and identity. To my surprise many religions, various models of consciousness, as well as some psychological frameworks, seemed to portray something similar.

The pyramid appears to have a story of the evolution of consciousness built into its very structure. At the top there is a formless, primordial force of a high frequency, often referred to as the fifth element of ether – the dynamic life force behind all matter. This etheric force is a universal concept found in all classical traditions, referred to as *chi*, *prana* or *ka*.

In the writings of Plato and the Pythagorean school in Greece it was kept hidden. Even though this fifth element is usually left out in modern materialistic science, it is similar to what is called the Quantum Field.

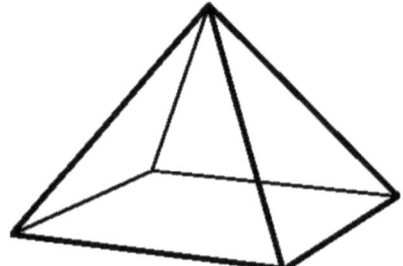

We live in an ocean of chi.
Some of it is yang, full of power and direction.
Some of it is yin, receptive and resting.
For the most part we are unaware of it
though it affects us on many levels.
Tom Kenyon

The frequency of this source energy has to be lowered in order to manifest in our material 3rd dimension. During this process the energy splits into a primary pair of opposites. These are equal to the concept of yin and yang, discovered by the sages of ancient China as they studied the patterns of nature.

The primary pair of opposites:
- an active part / energy in motion (warm / light – dry / firm)
- a passive part / potential energy (cold / heavy – damp / flexible)

Every force has these two complementary expressions of yin and yang. They are not static forces though, but continually transform into each other. The tension between these opposites works like a generator, which gives birth to energy.

The two opposite pairs give rise to a secondary pair of opposites:
- The heavy and flexible give rise to *water*.
- The light and flexible create *air*.
- Light and firm become *fire*.
- That which is heavy and firm make up *earth*.

This secondary pair of opposites form the base of the pyramid and are referred to as *the four basic elements*. These forces are important parts of philosophy, religion, medicine, mythology and psychology. In Sumer, where religion permeated every aspect of life, the four elements correlated with the most important gods: Anu, Enlil, Ninhursaga and Enki. The five elements are seen as the structure of creation in Tibetan cosmology and are found in the holy scriptures of India, like the Bhagavad Gita, as well as the philosophic concept behind Ayurvedic medicine. They are also an important part of Taoism and Traditional Chinese Medicine (TCM). Plato talked about the four tempers: Melancholic (water), sanguine (air), choleric (fire) and phlegmatic (earth). Hippocrates developed them into a medical theory and Carl Gustav Jung's work with four basic psychological functions are correlated to them. The four elements are also important parts of astrology and anthroposophy.

The elements are much more complex than personality types, though. They rather describe the processes behind different formative forces and are a more profound way of explaining the nature of life. Even though science might not support the elements as basic forces behind our physical world, it cannot take away the depth and wisdom behind systems like I Ching, TCM, astrology or Jung's theory of psychological functions.

As the elements continue to mix and grow in complexity, they form the 64 hexagrams described in *I Ching, the Book of Changes*, which is believed to be more than 3,000 years old. *The Gene Keys*, a system designed for personal transformation that maps our unique psycho-logical and spiritual makeup, is based on these universal codes, that are also mirrored in the 64 codons of our DNA.

The pyramid reveals that the stability of our identity (which can be seen as a sort of vehicle for our Soul or higher Self) depends on the balance of the four corners at its base. This means that as we explore and integrate the basic elements we can more easily embody and express our higher Self. In other words we need to learn how to recognize, and use, the inner forces that create the foundation of what we experience as identity.

(Colors and shapes help us do this, which is further explored in *The Art of Designing Identity*.)

To embody some kind of totality might not be possible, though. As humans beings in a 3D experience, some parts of us will always be partly hidden and projected onto the outer world. But if we are conscious of this process the complex interaction between our own psyche and the world around us becomes revealed. We begin to interpret experiences in our daily lives with curiosity and humility. We take ownership of how we interpret things that happen. Tolerance, patience and love grows, which in itself creates a different inner climate as well as a better world.

Natural Human Growth

A s human beings we go through different stages of growth. We all know that an infant who learns to walk first tries to stand up, then eventually takes a step or two, just to fall down endless times before it masters this new skill. While the 3-year-old would never ask you a hypothetical question, the 14-year-old loves to. Even though our ability to walk, or the development of our thinking, is encouraged by most parents, it is really an evolutionary drive, like an inbuilt program of growth, that is inherent in our species and that would come about even without coaxing.

Few would question that there are distinct developmental stages during childhood. But we seem to believe that we hit a magical milestone somewhere around our 20's and become "adults". It doesn't stop there, though. Rather than a fully formed stage, the adult is an evolving self, with a capacity to develop significantly.

Adult development theory has been around for several decades and recognizes distinct developmental stages in adults, where the same mechanics are at play:

- We are inspired by some new skill that can expand our life experience. Motivation is born.
- Failure and setbacks sometimes make us feel like giving up, but we persist in practicing this new skill.

- Eventually what we learn becomes a natural and integrated part of us.
- Once we have reached this place, what used to inspire and motivate us doesn't anymore. Our focus shifts to a new challenge and a new stage of growth.

Stages are necessary. We don't learn to walk at the same time as we try to figure out how letters become words. Our brain needs to grasp how to control and coordinate the body's limbs and muscles, and turn it into something we do automatically, before it can begin to process a different type of skill and a new level of complexity.

There are many theories of human growth. The ones I have valued the most in my own exploration have been humanistic, developmental and transpersonal psychology, since they added important facets to my understanding. Carl Gustav Jung's work on adult growth and collective consciousness also provided a lot of insights.

Many sources of ancient wisdom, that relate to human consciousness and its development, tend to focus more on energy systems and a symbolic language to describe these. This makes a lot of sense since the human psyche, and different levels of consciousness, are not something tangible that can easily be divided into parts, studied rationally and explained logically. It's a subconscious world of complex energetic processes that can be best perceived with our intuitive right-brain, a holistic approach and symbolic languages. If we are willing to put aside the different attempts at rationalizing psychological processes, as well as trying to squeeze them too tightly into linear progressions, we can discover, and learn to appreciate, concepts like different vibrations, channels of energy flow and frequency intervals.

As we attempt to describe these invisible and complex inner worlds, this kind of approach is definitely relevant. It is a way of looking at consciousness and human growth that is easily related to octaves in music and colors as fractions of light. Shapes and sacred geometry also fit perfectly into this way of relating to the psyche, since they also tell us, in a language beyond words, about human development and what it might mean to evolve and become more whole. Systems like I Ching and astrology also speak to us in a symbolic language.

When I tried to find a way to define different areas of growth in this book, I also leaned heavily on my personal experience of development. Looking back I could definitely distinguish various stages of growth related to different needs and motivations. Knowledge of one's own nature is also knowledge of human nature in general.

> We do not grow absolutely, chronologically.
> We grow sometimes in one dimension, and not in another; unevenly.
> We grow partially. We are relative.
> We are mature in one realm, childish in another.
> The past, present, and future mingle and pull us backward,
> forward, or fix us in the present.
> We are made up of layers, cells, constellations.
> *Anaïs Nin*

Various ways of looking at adult growth agree on these points:

- It is possible to detect different stages in our growth process.
- Rather than a linear progression it is more like the annual growth rings of a tree, where each new level adds something to what was already integrated.
- Development equals growing complexity.

There are also areas of dispute. Some psychologists mean that the need on a specific level must be met before we can move on to the next. Others question this and claim that we can satisfy needs on several levels at the same time. When it comes to clothes this is obvious – they can certainly protect us from cold winds at the same time as they help us fit into a certain societal group. So even if a specific need might be prioritized, several can be active at once while others might be neglected.

Let's look at these different stages, the specific needs they are related to and how clothes can help us fill those needs.

Basic Needs

W e have used some form of clothes – the simplest being fur, leaves and draped grass – since early on in the story of humanity. The ideal time to begin to use clothes for warmth would have been a million years ago, when early humanoids lost their body hair.

Gaining knowledge about the use of clothes is difficult since textiles, along with other organic materials, deteriorate quite rapidly. A genetic analysis of human body lice suggests that our use of different garments began between 83,000 to 170,000 years ago. The migration from Africa's warm climate (50,000-100,000 years back in time) increased our need for some kind of body protection, so by then clothes must have been necessary. Sewing needles of bone and ivory from 30,000 BC (40,000 BC according to some) confirm that by this time clothes were a common part of everyday life.

Our most basic human needs are air, water and food. A protected place to stay, as well as ways to protect our bodies, is another main physical requirement for human survival. To function optimally every living organism needs to maintain its inner physical and chemical conditions within certain limits. This is called *homeostasis*. When we are healthy our bodies have the ability to regulate these systems. If the conditions of our outer environment are too extreme, there is a risk of disturbance that might threaten our very survival. Most of us, who don't live in some kind of Eden with a perfect climate, need external aid to stay within these boundaries. This is where clothes come in. Different kinds of materials, made into fabrics and garments, can help regulate our internal balance when the climate we live in is too hot or cold, too dry or moist. They can form a protective barrier against water, wind, sand / dust and sun.

Another area of basic needs that clothes help us fill is related to safety. They can provide a sturdier 2nd skin to protect our own very sensitive skin from rough surfaces. This barrier between ourselves and the environment can shield us from rash-causing plants, insect bites (beekeeper gear), splinters and thorns. Garments that are specifically made for sport and other physical activities, such as padded knees or shoulders and motorcycle leathers, are also made to protect us from different kinds of risks.

Clothes can also keep toxic and infectious materials away from the body. Examples of clothes made as solutions to environmental hazards are space suits, air conditioned clothing, armor and diving suits. There is also high-visibility clothing with luminous reflector tape to help us be seen at night in traffic. Sometimes we are protected by not being seen, like in a war where we can wear uniforms with green or tan camouflage patterns.

On this basic physiological level clothes also fill functional needs. Two typical examples from the long list practical functions on clothes could be pockets, made to help us carry things along as we move around, and aprons that stop food from staining our ordinary clothes when we cook. Different garments can also satisfy a need for physical comfort. A cozy sweater to wrap around us or a soft shawl around one's neck can make us feel more at ease.

Most of us feel safer just by wearing clothes. How would you feel if you suddenly stood in a group of people without any clothes on? Probably embarrassed. Maybe scared, feeling very exposed. As vulnerable as can be. Even though having clothes on when we go about our everyday lives is not a universal habit, it's a social norm that we have been conditioned by. It has been internalized in our culture. With clothes on we have put up a kind of barrier to hide our most intimate parts, our innermost selves. We are in control of when, and with whom, we choose to remove these barriers.

Some cultures have very strictly regulated dress codes, especially for the female part of the population. The hijab or burka are supposed to be a way of protecting women. This is certainly true in the sense that not adhering to these rules can be connected to hazard in some parts of the world.

A Need to Belong

With the need to belong we move on to psychological needs that are connected to certain behavior patterns in our relationship to others. Whether we look at a smaller or larger group – it could be family, a group of friends, co-workers or the culture we live in – our need to belong is about feeling included and accepted. In our distant past being included in the group was necessary for our very survival, which is stored in the deepest recesses of our memory.

At the very beginning of our lives two essential psychological drives are competing; *attachment* and *authenticity*. To attach, and feel a sense of belonging, we need to be held and nurtured. But equally important is our need to be who we are, to develop trust in ourselves and our own gut feelings. In the best possible situation the profoundly important parent-child relationship provides the emotional support and intimacy we crave to become comfortable and feel safe, in our bodies as well as in our budding selves. We thus learn how to relate to ourselves and to others.

During the very first months or years of our lives we are fully authentic. We have access to an entire range of feelings and express what we feel without filters. But if we sense that our frustration, our need to cuddle or tireless exploration of the world is not appreciated, we are faced with a dilemma. If we continue to be ourselves fully our attachment might be threatened. Since our need to belong is so deeply tied to survival, we might begin to adapt and deny our authentic expression. We hide certain feelings, which begins to shape our budding personality. As we reach adolescence we might not even know what we really feel, and continue to believe that we need to behave in certain ways to be accepted and included. Awareness of this tension between attachment and authenticity is important.

The need to belong can also be met through clothes. We simply dress in a way that is similar to the group or culture we want to be included in and associated with. It is a silent and widely used way of saying: "I am similar to you, I belong to your group".

This is very obvious in the traditional dresses of many ethnic groups, like that of Sweden's indigenous people, the Sami. There are symbols in their garments to tell others about their gender, status and ancestors, as well as where they belong geographically. Similar codes are found in the traditional Kimono of Japan. In classical antiquity the dressing codes were also very clear. A lot of fabric in the outfit meant a high position, while less fabric signaled lower status. Certain details carried easily interpreted messages, like the color of a headdress, the length of the garment, the shawl around one's shoulders or a belt in a certain pattern. Contemporary fashions and dress codes might not be as clear, but are still an efficient way to tell others about the groups we are, or want to be, related to.

This need to belong is especially strong in adolescence and can, depending on the strength of peer pressure, even override physiological and security needs. It is not unusual to see teenagers in winter with a specific brand of sneakers that were made for warmer days, or young girls who expose so much of their bodies that their safety might be compromised in some situations. (For the record I adamantly believe that it's a basic human right to be safe regardless of how much of our bodies we choose to show. The fact that we are not remains though.)

Many would argue that they don't follow fashion. But even if we don't think we do, most adhere to dress codes to fit into a specific professional arena, or a group of people with similar interests. In today's informal world dress codes still determine, to a large extent, what we wear and when we wear it.

Esteem Needs

T he other psychological drive is our need for esteem. The word is derived from the Latin *aestimare*, which means to appraise, value, rate, weigh and estimate. There are several ways to gain worldly esteem and social recognition – through how powerful or successful we are, an interesting job title or how we look. All are tied to collective ideals and mindsets, and how we are seen and valued in the eyes of others.

The subtle language of fashion and dress codes provide us with wearable symbols of status and power. Even though the symbols vary depending on which group or culture we look at, clothing has been a weapon in people's struggle for social recognition for millennia. Dressing well by wearing highly valued designer clothes, being at the leading edge of fashion, or putting on an expensive suit to show rank and power, can build a strong persona that might help us feel seen and respected. Implicit dress codes even influence opportunities, while some might actually lose their jobs for refusing to adhere to these.

> One can make a gentleman from two yards of cloth.
> *Cosimo de Medici*

At this stage of development we are overly concerned by receiving appreciation, believing we need to be or look a certain way to get attention or validation. Depending on the result we either feel good or bad about ourselves. On the days when our clothes make us look really good, and we get positive attention, our self-confidence is boosted. This can satisfy us temporarily. It doesn't matter if we are aware that it's only on a superficial level, it still compensates for cracks in our self-esteem.

Constantly fed with images of people with "perfect" bodies, hair, makeup and clothes, we can easily get stuck in patterns of insecurity if we compare ourselves to these impossible ideals. Too many of us have a sense of being flawed – too thin, too heavy, too old – of not looking "good enough". Feeling like we have nothing to put on even though our wardrobes are crammed with clothes.

As long as we have a subconscious belief that designer clothes, fashion or certain dress codes are the keys to self-confidence we will keep buying and dressing in them, even though what we are really looking for is a solution to our internal issues. The garment industry will keep supplying what we believe we need and, in a sense, exploit this desire for social recognition. But it is really up to us to recognize these signs and to begin to look closer at our own lack of self-esteem. Deep down we all know that the confidence that can be boosted by a cool and flawless visual appearance has little to do with who we really are. True self-esteem lives at the core of our identity, as a cognitive and emotional appraisal of our own unique qualities and innate value. It has nothing to do with how we perform, what we achieve, or how we look and dress. Still so many of us lack this solid and unshakable confidence.

People with a healthy self-esteem usually have less need for a lot of clothes. Unless they truly enjoy their beauty that is, because clothes can, of course, also be a creative way of expressing our true Self. The vital question, that no one but ourselves knows the answer to, is: Are you dressing to live up to ideals or to gain prestige? Does your ego want to stick out and distinguish yourself from the crowd as creative and different? Or do you dress because it's a pleasure and an inner need to express your uniqueness?

The most endangered species on earth is the human soul.
Many try to stand in one world only, the world of the collective culture,
thereby experiencing a sense of standing outside the true self.
Clarissa Pinkola Estés

The developmental psychologist Robert Kegan calls this stage *The Socialized Mind*, since the mindsets, beliefs and ideals of the people around us is what's most important. According to him this is the stage where we find most people in our culture at the present time. Abraham Maslow, who was also a developmental psychologist, called all of the stages we have looked at until now "deficiency needs". According to him the individual would feel anxious and tense if these needs are not met, and would be driven to go on seeking what he or she is looking for. I don't believe this to be true. If our need for esteem had to be filled before we could find the motivation to focus on higher needs, I doubt if adult growth would exist. A simple realization that we want to find true self-esteem is what opens us up to further growth.

Aesthetic Needs

E very stage of growth brings out a new human facet associated with some kind of expansion of what we call identity. In order to evolve we need to stretch our boundaries to include larger parts of ourselves. As we do, we grow in complexity.

The earlier needs, born out of deficiency, are soon to be replaced by growth needs. This fourth level can be seen as a kind of gateway to these higher levels. Aesthetic needs emerge with a new motivation to seek for a closer connection to our heart and soul.

A new bond is formed with unconditional love and a beauty that goes beyond cultural values. In this process our connection to nature is reinforced. We begin to immerse ourselves in nature's beauty and open up to be re-energized by it. As we do, something in us starts to shift. Beauty can be truly transformative in this way. These kinds of experiences, that touch our heart and soul, are necessary in order to evolve, since it results in a sense of intimacy with nature and the earth, and at the same time to deeper parts of ourselves.

This new relationship to our heart and to nature shifts our perception of beauty. Our aesthetic sense becomes more refined. Carefully crafted objects, or fabrics with beautiful patterns and colors, begin to touch a deeper cord in us. Our need to beautify our lives grows and we are more able to appreciate the beauty in the world around us on a daily basis.

> There are cultural norms and then there are deeper laws,
> rivers of deep wisdom that beckon us back to who we really are
> beneath the roles that we've been taught to play.
> *Claire Dubois*

The connection to clothes on this level is pretty obvious. As we open up to the sometimes overwhelming beauty of nature, there is no way we can keep our blinders on to how badly it is affected by our overconsumption of clothes, to the enormous waste of resources as well as all the toxic waste that comes with it. We begin to care deeply about the state of nature and might engage in questions regarding sustainability. Fabrics made out of natural and renewable materials are favored and we look for recycling and eco-friendly options in production as well as garments.

Along with this new heartfelt sense of caring there is also compassion and empathy. As we care more about our fellow humans in the world, we can no longer tolerate the exploitation of textile laborers.

Instead of following cultural beauty standards, or caring about what somebody else thinks is beautiful, we begin to follow our own heart. This new sense of aesthetics might make us marvel at the beauty of a well-worn and patched pair of trousers or the playful dance of colors in a shirt pattern. We begin to understand and appreciate the importance of quality, and focus more on giving than on getting. This can lead us to dress in order to share beauty, joy, creativity and presence – a stark contrast to the previous drive of asking for attention.

Inner Balance

I n the mid-20th century humanistic psychologists like Carl Gustav Jung, Roberto Assagioli and Abraham Maslow presented new psychological models that recognized higher levels of human growth. They used the term *self-actualization* to describe the blossoming of our natural gifts and innate talents.

Even though most would desire a blossoming of their true potential, the path that leads there includes more than making simple improvements. It requires us to take a step back, look at our identity from a neutral standpoint and acknowledge our need for inner growth. We are usually quite unaware that there is a difference between our personality and what we call the Self before this need is awakened. But as this awareness grows there is a dawning realization that we might be more than the person we believed ourselves to be. This insight is crucial, since it opens up the possibility that we have yet to grow into the person we were meant to be. We make a conscious choice to participate in our own evolution.

Regardless of what ignites this motivation, a whole new perspective of ourselves opens up as we take our first steps on this path of growth. In the beginning there is usually a gap between how we see ourselves as opposed to how others see us, as well as between different parts of our identity. So the first thing we need to look at is this gap. How do I express myself? Why does my persona look the way it does? Are there parts of myself that I prefer to hide? In this process we begin to see our personality in a new light. The face we present to the world might hide what lies behind it - who we really are deep down at the core.

The experiential part of this development involves beginning to peek behind the armor of our Ego. As we proceed, we become increasingly aware of the different parts that make it up, and begin to discern which parts dominate and which are suppressed. We start to explore how we have been conditioned by our family and culture, and examine the fear, anger, pride or shame behind our automatic reactions. We evaluate our own behaviors as well as the dynamics of our inner and outer relationships, and begin to rediscover parts of us that have been hidden or denied for different reasons.

It's not an easy ride. Since there are reasons as to why certain aspects of ourselves have been put aside or hidden, it can also be painful. Many would do anything to avoid facing themselves. But sooner or later we come to a point where circumstances in our lives tell us that we need to, and sometimes even have to, change and grow. The rewards of a richer life are definitely worth the efforts required.

> Yesterday I was clever, so I wanted to change the world.
> Today I am wise, so I am changing myself.
> *Rumi*

One of the most important processes in this stage of growth is to balance our conscious traits and their hidden counterparts. As we search inside ourselves for the polar opposites to the characteristics we are most strongly identified with, it can be important to learn more about them. Why have they been suppressed? Have we simply been conditioned to see one pole as better than the other, or are traumatic experiences involved?

The psychological term *projection* describes a defense mechanism. It makes us interpret the parts that we are ashamed of, and deny in ourselves, as belonging to somebody else. If our vulnerability is dis-owned we might look down on those who show these characteristics. If being lazy was seen as a strongly negative trait as we grew up, people who are more laid back might really upset us. We dump the shame on them, so to speak. If we are scared of our own power, we might idolize, or fear, somebody who expresses this quality. As long as we are driven by these projections that trigger automatic emotional reactions and drama, we are ruled by our conditioned personality.

The habit of seeing things as good or bad splits the innate wholeness of our identity. We become like a broken mirror where the shattered pieces are sorted in two piles. As we learn to take a step back, and observe things from a neutral standpoint, we can begin to heal this fragmentation. There isn't such a thing as good or bad, there is only conscious and unconscious, as well as different perspectives on personal traits.

To include hidden parts in our conscious identity involves embracing them. We learn to truly appreciate vulnerability. We begin to love the recuperation of lazy moments. If we are overly generous we find our balance when we learn to also appreciate being thrifty. In this process we become free to act in a non-judgmental way and learn to adapt more easily to different situations. As we learn to hold the polarities inside us we become more creative. Life becomes more harmonious.

This balancing act is not a journey with an end. It is rather a refined habit of exploring and contemplating what we experience as identity, a continuous process where we discover and unwind patterns, balance counterparts, heal traumatic experiences and bring our emotional body to rest. Eventually it becomes a state of being. The big change involved is a shift in identification – from a personality that is defined by a few specific characteristics, to a larger concept of what and who we are – an aware Ego as a vehicle to express our inner Self.

An innate part of us emerges, and begins to take more space, as we travel along this path. It's a silent observer who, from a neutral stand-point, constantly registers the thoughts and feelings of our fragmented inner parts, along with the interaction between them. This part helps us gain the insights and awareness needed in order to weave together the disintegrated parts to a growing wholeness.

There is also a cognitive part in this stage of development – a natural drive to expand the use of our intelligence through being curious; questioning, exploring and discovering. We can actually train our minds to be more flexible, to see different perspectives of a subject and to discern overall patterns. This helps us gain a better understanding of complexity, not only inside ourselves but also around us. Since no cognitive growth is possible if we think we already know and understand things, this is directly related to having an open mind.

An important part of this process is to begin to question the prevailing cultural narrative that was so crucial to follow when we were driven by esteem needs. We evaluate our own beliefs and ideals as well as how we have been conditioned to think. As our mind becomes more independent we can question things we have taken for granted. We begin to shape our own understanding of the world instead of allowing it to be shaped by certain authorities and the cultural setting of which we are a part.

We also begin to look critically at the basic assumptions we have about this thing we call identity. We are no longer defined by our relationships, our jobs or culture, but embark on a journey of defining ourselves. We can explore our thoughts and feelings and take responsibility for them. We realize that we are always changing.

To become "the most that we can be" might sound grand, but this is definitely not the aim. Our journey towards actualizing our potential is about doing what we need to do in order to feel fulfilled, about finding our natural way of expression. Our passion. To some this might mean being a good parent, achieving some athletic feat or being a source of integrity in our work place. But it can also be things we are used to perceive as more grand, like creating music or inventing something. Following our heart, regardless of how it looks to the outer world, is key. This might mean the artist who has never made a profit from their art, but who continues to paint because it's fulfilling. It might be the person who finds joy in achieving mastery in a niche hobby, or the employee at a nonprofit who uses their skills to improve the lives of others.

As awareness grows our definition of success is redefined. We realize that it isn't equated with a high income or how important we can become. Receiving positive attention from others, "succeeding" or "doing something grand" belongs to the level of needs that is driven by esteem. We have now become more humble. Our new definition of success is when we are at peace, treat others with compassion, live a balanced life filled with love and growth, and align with the mission of our Self. The "grandest" thing might be to dare be transparent and vulnerable, and to recognize our own flawed nature so that we can forgive others for their imperfections.

> Some days I am goddess.
> Some days I am wild child.
> And some days I am a fragile mess.
> Most days I am a bit of all three.
> But every day I am here, trying.
> *S.C. Lourie*

We begin to dress for our own sake when we unplug from the need of seeking approval from others. A great first step on our path to Self-actualization is to use our wardrobe to get more clear about our personality, ego and persona. (See *The Wardrobe Speaks* in part III for input.)

As we become accustomed to a holistic perspective clothes take on a different meaning, and become priceless tools on our path to find inner balance. A new relationship between the different parts of our identity and the dressed body emerges. We learn to be more observant and mindful of how colors, shapes and visible patterns are combined to express different traits. As we become more open to intuit how we are affected by them, they can serve as tools to strengthen parts of us that are weak, awaken parts that have been denied or neglected and balance the extremes of our psychological make-up. Even mending clothes becomes more meaningful. Visible repair can actually be a way of embellishing our own cracks and flaws, of being proud of how we have grown from stitching ourselves together.

Integration

A new stage of growth, with a different challenge, begins to motivate us when we have become more acquainted with the different parts of our inner world. As we continue to refine and calibrate our psyche as a vehicle for the Self or Soul, we are now primarily focused on integrating polar opposites.

So what is the difference between a balanced personality, that consists of many parts that we are aware of and value, and one that has been integrated? Even though our dominant belief system has split polarities into incompatible extremes that are in conflict, we tend to forget is that there is really a simultaneous push and pull between them. This is why they are so dynamic. Opposite poles are inherently attracted to each other, like magnetism. As we saw in the concept of Yin and Yang one wouldn't exist without a balanced interchange with the other.

There are many opposite poles in our psyche and we all have our individual setup that we need to explore. As we enter this integrating process we often lack the experience of how to use counterparts in a dynamic balance. But as the process proceeds it becomes increasingly difficult to separate one from the other. Along with the realization that we can't be truly powerful without an equal amount of vulnerability a new quality, that includes both, seems to emerge. The same thing happens as we become aware that an intellectual challenge cannot be solved without intuitive insights, or that we can actually love and hate the same person. Grief and joy can become so close that they actually feel the same. We stop seeing them as incompatible parts. Opposite poles become inter-woven forces that constantly interact in a state of dynamic balance. We can hold a perspective where there is no contradiction or split between opposites, nor between competing belief systems. A result of this reconciliation of opposites is that it automatically invites the Self onto our inner arena.

Some of you might have met a person who is very feminine and at the same time very masculine. (Note that I refer to psychological integration and not sexual orientation.) There is this new quality that makes it difficult to define a person's traits. They have become integrated. If one of the extreme poles is needed in a situation, it takes the lead. The inner counterparts have become like a close-knit team in constant interaction. It's the same with any major opposing force, like being active – passive or receptive – insusceptible.

> Recognize this kaleidoscope,
> this spectrum that you are - this whole world within.
> You are at the very center of it.
> *Lee Harris*

As I tried to find the right word as a counterpart to receptive, something interesting happened that is so typical of our predominant mindset. We are so used to a standpoint of imbalance and polarization that a counterpart to a word usually has a negative bias. The opposite of generous is often described as tight-fisted or greedy. As I search for a neutral word for the opposite trait, I come up with thrifty or economical. The opposite to this word is usually not generous but wasteful.

In the process of integration we learn something imperative: One pole is never better than the other. It always depends on the situation. If we lean towards a belief that one is slightly superior, it is simply a sign that we are not yet balanced and integrated.

The final fusion of inner polarities are the counterparts of yin and yang, or feminine and masculine, that we all carry inside of us. Mastery is the ability to combine the focus of the yang with the receptivity of the yin. Two very different kinds of existing, relating and knowing merge. On the path to this humble space at the center we gain clarity and wisdom. As we experience the world with a non-dual consciousness we can fully identify with our Self or Soul. We are linked to our wise and untamed Self, that emerges from the realm of mystery, dreams, and shadows. As a sense of being truly embodied grows life becomes an interesting weave of simple complexity.

Unity

B ecoming more balanced and integrated helped us find inner wholeness. In this process our timeless core essence becomes more embodied. Our consciousness expands and we begin to perceive glimpses of unity. Instead of being confined to a fragmented sense of self made of different parts and traits, we can freely move back and forth to experience a dimension where there is a sense of flow – where our experience of duality, and boundaries between parts, are partly dissolved. With the return to our timeless, sovereign core a social mask is no longer needed. We become more transparent and express ourselves authentically.

Transpersonal psychology integrates the spiritual and transcendent aspects of the human experience with the framework of modern psychology. It is defined as experiences in which our sense of self extends beyond the individual and personal to encompass wider aspects of life.

Transcendence is such an intriguing word though. It implies that we, at some point that is beyond our control, are mysteriously moved to a higher plane of existence. Mystics and spiritual teachings seem to confirm that we actually do enter into a new dimension as our personality is integrated with our higher Self or Soul. To grasp how this reality will be felt before we have actually experienced it is, of course, impossible. If we return to our metaphor of the larvae, there is no way for it to grasp the perspective, nor the experience or abilities, of the butterfly.

Having reached this multi-dimensional nature means that our unique core qualities are expressed and that our full potential can be manifested. Our identity has become the perfectly attuned vehicle for our Soul, and our resources are directed and used by its vision and intention. We feel more connected to something larger and more encompassing – humanity, Earth and the universe – and are driven by a need to contribute, a longing to be of service.

> The universe gains a novel and irreducible
> perspective of itself through our being.
> We get to play our part in the revealing of that.
> *Andre Duqum*

Identified with our Self our core qualities become obvious. If these are also expressed through the clothes we wear, the inner and outer merge and become congruent. Visual fabrics patterns for clothes can help us embody and express our unique combination of inner qualities.

Since the essential core that we call our Soul is eternal, clothes on this level need to have a more timeless quality. I don't refer to simplicity or minimalism as a style, but a genuine return to simple, authentic clothing expressions. We might use robes and original garments that are really comfortable to wear, with no restrictions to the flow of energy through our being. Or maybe we will invent new genuine styles. Timeless beauty is nourishment for our soul. It thrives as our bodies are wrapped in it.

PART III

The Art of Designing Identity

There are deeper values in art than aesthetic ones.
Colors and shapes are living forces,
which we can learn to use consciously
to develop our personality.
Roberto Assagioli

What we wear matters. With a new awareness of different stages of human growth, and how these are connected to clothes, we can begin to look at what it means to dress with intention. To become true artists at tweaking and fine-tuning the different facets of identity, we only need to learn about the tools at hand and practice using them.

As a culture we seem to have forgotten that colors, shapes, patterns and styles are actually a language. It surpasses the traditional language centers and tells us about a world of energy and force fields. Its forgotten letters formed by different color hues, syllables made up of a variation of shapes along with words of style, are a yin language. One that is read and spoken fluently by the right side of our brains. The skill of using this language to communicate with our inner worlds can be reawakened.

On a personal level this helps us explore the attitudes and behaviors our personality is composed of. It provides tools to help us move towards inner balance and wholeness. For the professional it opens up a whole new world of possibilities to design clothes for the future, where the language of energy is an integral part.

The Wardrobe Speaks

Our clothing style is intricately connected to how we see ourselves, as well as the personal parts we feel comfortable in showing the people around us. Certain colors, fabric patterns and styles also shape the content of our wardrobes. Those garments make us feel at ease. We know who we are and how to express ourselves, and don't have to ponder the question: "Who am I?" every morning before we get dressed.

As long as an unaware Ego is running the show, "good" clothes are those that help us get the kind of attention we want from others. It might be to look cool, strict or powerful, to follow dress codes or send clear signals that we don't care at all about what impression we make. It might also be to hide who we are, partly or entirely. What to keep in mind is that an unaware Ego always tries to cover up, or compensate for, our insecurities.

As a new level of needs begins to motivate us, our clothes take on a different meaning. From the perspective of the Self our best clothes are those that will help us expand our identity, so that we can begin to embody and express our core essence. A necessary first step when our need for Inner Balance, the first of the growth needs, is awakened is *self-knowledge* – more clarity about our personality traits and the characteristics we tend to identify with. Since there is a direct correlation between the colors, patterns and styles in our wardrobe and our primary inner parts, the wardrobe becomes a great guide on this journey.

So put on a pair of imaginary spectacles with a neutral perspective, open its doors, take a good look at the garments inside and ponder these (or similar) questions:

- What is the first overall impression of this wardrobe?
- Is it neat and organized or chaotic?
- Is the wardrobe colorful or neutral?
- Do any specific colors dominate (black, blue, different shades of some specific color)?
- Are there any printed or woven patterns, and if so, what kind (checkered, striped, floral)?
- What kind of fabric qualities dominate (heavy or lightweight, sturdy or soft)?
- Is any kind of garment overly represented (lots of shirts, mostly trousers, only dresses)?
- What kind of styles do you see (strict, super-relaxed, cool, sensual, romantic)?
- In which of these garments are you most comfortable?
- Are there clothes you rarely use, and if so, what kind of style (and trait) do they represent?

To look at what our wardrobe expresses can bring important clues about personality traits that we might not be fully aware of. So taking the time to really look at what's there – as well as what isn't there – can be really valuable.

Once we gain an overall perspective of the various traits and ideals we are obviously identified with, we can begin to take a closer look at our personality. What specific traits did we take on through conditioning and family values? Are there clothes that tend to hide our core characteristics? Which garments help us express what feels authentic?

As we begin to look at what our clothes, and ways to dress, say about ourselves, we also tend to look at the clothing expression of others from a different perspective. Since it is impossible to know why other people dress the way they do, releasing any judgement we might have about somebody else's clothing expression is important. Yes, clothes are an expression of who we are, but our reasons for dressing the way we do, and the choices of colors and patterns we make, can be more or less conscious. They depend on our level of self-awareness.

- Some are strictly ruled by societal values, dress codes or fashion.
- A person's clothing style can be an expression of their conditioned personality traits.
- People on a journey of inner development might use their clothes as tools for inner growth.
- Some have become conscious of their soul qualities and are trying to find an expression for those.

Figuring out our personality traits, and raising our awareness of who we are, is an ongoing process. As our characteristics become more clear our garments are transformed into great tools for inner growth on our path to inner balance and integration. But using them consciously requires knowledge about the language of colors, shapes, patterns and clothing styles, though. So let's begin to practice!

A Language of the Psyche

W e already know that everything, in its essence, is energy. A feeling, or thought, has a frequency, a vibration and some kind of pattern. Energies can be distinguished by what we interpret as sounds and rhythms, images, body movement and dance, visual patterns and colors, just to name a few. They express the subconscious realities that cannot be understood, nor clearly expressed, through our intellect. These expressions form the universal language of the psyche and also affect our energy and our state of consciousness.

What we surround ourselves with takes on a new importance when we become fully aware of the fact that we are continuously affected by the large amounts of subconscious information around us. Since the garments we wear are closest to our body and energy field, they become especially important. We might begin to ask ourselves some different questions: Are the colors light or heavy? Is there flow in the fabric patterns? Are the materials made of natural fibers that help my body breathe? Do the garments allow full movement?

To refine our perception of clothes, so they can be used as tools, we need to learn a language that only appears, and begins to make sense, if we scale clothes down to their very essence. What is left as we do are colors, shapes, patterns (which are a combination of colors and shapes in some kind of repetition and movement) as well as clothing styles.

Figuring out the basics of this language was a somewhat tricky process for me since there are many readymade templates for interpreting colors. I remember my deep frustration early on when I explored ways to relate colors and shapes to our psyche. The different models for color interpretation never seemed to agree and seemed like very mental categorizations. Knowing that these energetic languages are not something we can understand on a purely logical level, and that a deeper way of experiencing them is needed, I decided to use my own designer's eye, as well as my intuition, as my base and to never accept interpretations that were not in line with my own gut feeling. I needed a lot of practice and personal experience to begin to understand this language of inner worlds, but with perseverance it began to make sense.

The following sections are an overview of the essential languages behind clothes. The first step is to learn two new alphabets; that of colors and shapes. To become truly skilled we also need to practice their specific grammar.

Our Energy Field

E very living organism on this planet is surrounded by an electromagnetic field that is constantly affected by other energies. Before we begin to zoom in on the specifics of colors, shapes, patterns and styles, it can be helpful to take a quick look at the highly complex human energy field, since it explains the close connection between colors, different emotions and states of mind.

Contemporary medical science has focused on the physical and chemical aspects of the human body, while another part of it has remained more hidden. Along with a growing interest for the human electromagnetic body, a number of researchers have begun to thoroughly investigated it. In 1994 a group of scientists began to use the word *biofield* to describe the energy that surrounds the human body. Initially the research was limited by a lack of equipment that was sensitive enough, but technological advancements have now made it possible to explore the human electromagnetic field more accurately. So far we know that it is composed of a series of electric, magnetic, and electromagnetic fields.

The biofield is often referred to as the *aura*. Other cultures, especially the ancient Indian and Vedic traditions, have described it extensively. People with the extra sensory perception of clairvoyance can see the aura and usually interpret it as colors that display our dominant feeling tone as well as bursts of emotions.

Light is a thing that cannot be reproduced
but must be represented by something else – by color.
Paul Cezanne

Everything we can perceive in the material world is energy in different states of density. So are we. Our physical body is the densest part of us, while the more subtle field around it consists of different layers. This gives us the ability to exist on several dimensions simultaneously.

Closest to our physical body there is a field of around half an inch called *the etheric body*, which stores our subconscious. Outside of the etheric field we find *the emotional body* and then *the mental body*, each consisting of a gradually finer substance. There are more, even subtler fields outside of these that connect us to higher dimensions. The ones mentioned are those that are part of our conditioned self and that gives rise to the personality. The emotional and mental body changes along with our emotions, thoughts and overall energy. There is also constant interaction between these fields. Negative thoughts lead to negative feelings, which eventually affect our physical body. If there is pain in our body it also affects our feelings and thoughts.

The term *chakra* (which means wheel in Sanskrit) refers to spinning vortices which are like energetic structures in the anatomy of our body's subtle energy. The seven lower chakras are connected to main glands or nerve clusters in our physical body, where the energy is transformed and directed to different organs. This explains why keeping our energy in balance is very important to our physical, emotional as well as mental well-being. Each chakra is also related to one of the seven colors of the rainbow.

There is a lot of information available for those who wish to know more about the aura and the chakra system. In this context we only need some basic knowledge to understand the connection between colors and our own energy.

A Language of Light

C olors are are a huge subject that is relevant in many different fields – from science, politics and social codes to visual signals in our daily lives, aesthetics in interior design, clothes or art and energy medicine, to name just a few. Colors can also relate to different levels of experience, from the purely concrete to an expression of moods and emotions, as well as magical or spiritual experiences.

Depending on age, gender, cultural conditioning as well as personal disposition, we experience colors very differently. To some they have deep significance while they are barely noticed by others. The entire spectra of fields and levels they span has deep relevance to us since, as human beings, we are also related to all of these. The different color hues and shades are a subtle way to describe this range of experiences.

From a scientific perspective colors are fractions of light; the small part of the spectrum of electromagnetic radiation that our human eyes can discern. We perceive the various frequencies as different color hues. But our eyes play tricks on us. A red sweater is actually every color except red. The sweater absorbs all the other color frequencies while red is reflected, which is what we see.

On a day-to-day level colors are a deeply integrated part of our society, and our instinctive responses to them can be vital to our survival. Instinctively we all know that there is some kind of warning in red signs, and that green tells us it is safe to proceed. Shopping for food we are usually quite unconscious of how color signals are used to lure us into buying things. In politics these codes are more obvious. Throughout history colors have also been used to a large extent to show social status. Even though it isn't as common in present time there are quite a lot of examples where we are used to relate certain colors to specific societal roles.

When people are asked what colors are to them, the most common answer, besides aesthetics, is that they express feelings. We amplify different moods in our homes with colors and color combinations. Bright or deep red nuances might be used to create warmth and stimulate outgoing activities in our living room. To surround us with tranquillity blue can be the dominant color. We also dress in different colors and shades depending on how we feel and how we want others to feel when they meet us.

If we look at colors from a psychological standpoint, many studies have examined their influence on human behavior and emotions. A large area of research has been to explore how they can be used in different environments, like prisons, schools or restaurants, to affect people's emotional states in various ways, for instance to make them feel calmer or stimulated in different ways. Different colored lights are also used to affect the growth of plants as well as the hormonal balance of animals.

Even though Western medicine uses X-ray, laser, infrared and ultraviolet light, as well as light therapy for depression, colors are still not widely accepted for their healing abilities. The importance of light and colors for our health and well being is slowly gaining acceptance though. We are rediscovering that certain glands in the body are stimulated by different frequencies of light, something shamans and mystics have known for thousands of years. Different fields of energy medicine are also fast becoming accepted practices and many believe that future medicine will be one of frequencies.

A color is not something concrete that we can touch. It is transient and changes with perception, light and the characteristics of the material that reflects it. Even though they are part of our daily lives, they exist in a realm between what is real and what isn't. They invite us into a world of vibrations.

Many also see colors as something magical. A rainbow in the sky can bring up a feeling of awe and inspiration. Even if our rational mind might remind us that what we perceive is a refraction of light through water droplets, the feeling of witnessing something supernatural might persist. Myth tells us that God put the rainbow in the sky as a sign of his alliance with every living creature on earth, and that the goddess Iris is a messenger between heaven and earth. In a way this is true; color is a non-verbal communication between the conscious mind and deeper parts of us, between our inner and outer worlds.

> Color provokes a psychic vibration.
> Color hides a power still unknown but real,
> which acts on every part of the human body.
> *Wassily Kandinsky*

Research has shown that our eyes can distinguish approximately 10 million different colors, even though the ability to discern shades and hues vary a lot between different people. This ability is usually more evolved in women, but can be developed through practice.

Since every color is so abstract and complex, color concepts are often vague. Words can merely try to reflect their quality. So how can a vibration best be described? Let's temporarily disregard scientific explanations, as well as our personal experience of colors, and simply focus on how we see them. As we do, we realize that we don't even see them in the same way. If you say bright blue I might have an association to a color shade that is very different from what you had in mind. Just saying red or green isn't enough. We need a language for color perception and several systems can help us with this. Since the correlation between colors and human emotions is important in this book, I have chosen one that makes this translation easy – The Natural Color System (NCS) developed by the Scandinavian Color Institute. In this system colors are defined by three values:

HUE
A percentage value between two of the colors red, yellow, green or blue.

BRIGHTNESS
How light or dark the color is.

SATURATION
The intensity of the color.

(NOTE: Due to different printing methods international readers might not have a copy of the book where these images, and a few others, are in color. If so you can visit my blog at metamorfos.se. In the posts about colors you can find these or similar images.)

If you use some kind of computer software for image processing, you probably know that you can choose between RGB, CMYK and HSB (sometimes HSL for lightness) when you want to adjust the color in an image. HSB (hue, saturation, brightness) corresponds with the NCS system.

Let's take a closer look at these three and how they can be translated to human experience.

Color Hues

The hue is what gives a color its basic name, like blue or yellow. It also describes how it is related to the other colors. Depending on the purpose of using them there are different ways of presenting them visually. In an art class they are often divided into primary colors – red, yellow and blue – since these can be mixed to create the secondary colors. At other times the primary colors are named red, yellow, green and blue.

There are also different ways of showing the entirety of colors; stacked on top of each other (which is based on their different frequencies) with red at the bottom and purple at the top, or as a color wheel, where red meets purple.

Who can say for certain exactly what green or red is, though? Since there is a gradual shift of color hues (or frequency) it is impossible to know exactly where a color begins or ends. Defining the hue of a color is about looking at its dominant wavelength.

The seven defined colors of the rainbow – red, orange, yellow, green, turquoise blue, indigo blue and purple – correspond to the chakra system in our human biofield. Since this way of looking at color hues can help us understand the connection between colors, different areas of life as well as certain emotions, it is the approach to colors chosen for this book. Hopefully this can help clarify how they affect us on deeper levels.

Color Brightness

The degree of light in any given hue is what we refer to as color brightness. The less light, the more dense, heavy or grounded the hue feels, while more light makes it feel more open and light. Both ends of this polarity can be good or bad, which is easier to grasp when we compare them to octaves in music that are so evident on a piano. The high notes are not better than the low, they simply have a different character.

To understand how light affects the quality of a color hue, and how it is related to the human psyche, we need to begin by looking at black and white that, in a technical sense, are not really colors. What we call black is the total absence of color. The surface appears black because it absorbs all color frequencies. White, on the other hand, absorbs none but reflects them all.

White is usually seen as purity and perfection – as something unattainable. It tells us about innocence and an openness to impressions, which are the qualities of a person with an enhanced sensitivity and thin boundaries to the outer world.

On the negative side a light color can add a quality of naivety, gullibility and escapism, like a person who floats above the challenges of life – someone with a "spiritual bypass", a term introduced in the 1980s by John Welwood. He was a Buddhist teacher and psychotherapist, and described the tendency to use spiritual ideas and practices to avoid facing unresolved issues, psychological wounds, and/or unfinished developmental tasks.

Black reflects integrity, authority and power, with clear boundaries towards the world. It's a quality that is hard, tough and capable of dealing with issues or obstacles in the midst of reality. A dark color can also emit a secretive inclination, bring a fascination for the unknown, the mystical, and help us look at what is hiding behind the surface of things.

On the downside black can be experienced as a negative and critical attitude that is insensitive to, and fails to acknowledge, the more subtle qualities in life. The tendency to put up boundaries can shut people out and make personal relationships more difficult.

The concept of light and dark is very complex. Collectively we are programmed to equate black with "bad" things, while white is used to portray the divine. Everybody knows that angels are white, while witches are black, right? And the devil will definitely arrive in black clothes. We use expressions like "healing white light", "dark evil forces", "a black book" and "the black sheep of the family", which further clarifies our general bias regarding these opposites.

Even if there might be an "absolute" regarding good and evil, it is less complex when we see it from a psychological viewpoint. One way of looking at light and dark is conscious versus unconscious. What we are aware of on one hand and what is unknown on the other. From this point of view it is easier to see that none is better than the other. With a good communication between conscious and unconscious everything is fine and our energy is flowing. An interesting thing to take into consideration is that if we suppress feelings, these unconscious energies can affect our psyche and health in a negative way. It can also express in negative ways.

Black is often connected to the feminine. It has tremendous power but, as we have seen in earlier chapters, deeply ingrained cultural values and a long history of being repressed and belittled in patriarchal culture, has twisted this energy into something that is feared.

At times we might need to be reminded of the many good things about darkness. Organic waste is transformed into nurturing compost in the dark. A seed cannot grow without it and the human fetus develops in the dark womb. It would also be impossible to see light without darkness.

The differences in how we perceive the opposites of black and white depends on our individual perspective. So what is your own relationship to this inner polarity? Do light or dark colors dominate in your wardrobe?

Color Saturation

Gray appears in the gradual shift between light/white and dark/black. The different gray shades express various degrees of neutrality or impartiality. From a psychological standpoint a gray color describes a personality trait of being neutral, of not taking a stand. These characteristics make good diplomatic mediators. But certain shades of gray can also be cold and hard, and create a mood that is quite devoid of life force, feelings and colors.

The saturation of a color tells us about the intensity or purity of the hue. 100% saturation means that there is no addition of gray, which makes a color intense and vivid. A hue with very low saturation looks gray with a barely detectable hint of the color hue.

If we translate saturation to a psychological language, it tells us about the intensity of different emotional states. A low saturation in a color can thus be interpreted as a low intensity of emotional energy and that the specific phase of the energetic process is not very strong.

Three Faces of Color

T he gradual shift from one color hue to another is the visual expression of an energetic process, a transition from one state – an attitude or mindset – to another. These can be divided into three overall phases. Even though all of us have the ability to shift between these three states, most will feel more at home in one of them, which provides important clues to our self-knowledge.

Your RED face – impulse for action
You are active and vital. The outer world and everyday reality is your primary focus and identification. Your energy flows outwards, is applied to the environment and brings immediate results. You react strongly and spontaneously to outside stimulation. Performance is important.

In this mode, you are not good at controlling your energy. You can go too far. You may begin projects full of enthusiasm, but can waste energy in euphoria when you succeed or get completely burnt out. You also tend to overestimate yourself.

All red, orange and yellow color hues (often favorite colors for extroverts) are expressions of this phase of the energetic process.

Your GREEN face – concentration and consolidation
The balancing point between the two opposite poles (of red and blue) now gathers momentum and slows things down. You become aware that energy is not unlimited and that you must learn how to use it. You begin

to avoid speculation, start taking responsibility and remove anything superfluous from your life.

A sense of reality is developed as well as the ability to follow things through. This is a stage of realistic awareness of your own abilities and limitations. Projects can be realized and made productive. Security is your main motivation. But, if the flow is stuck in this stage, your energy might stagnate.

Different hues of green (from yellowish green to grass green and bluish green) are connected to this stage. The quality is neither active nor passive, neither outgoing nor introvert, but stable. There is balance and growth.

Your BLUE face – withdrawal and change

The energy now turns inward, to your inner life. Even though you might still be involved in external activities these are not your main motivation. Introspection and contemplation has become more important than the outer world. Experiences are analyzed and processed, and you accept the consequences of actions, become aware of unrealized dreams. This leads to self-awareness and maturation. But if you lean too heavily on this end of the spectrum, it can lead to passivity, resignation or depression.

Turquoise blue, indigo blue and violet (colors that are preferred by introverts) symbolize this phase.

At the end of the blue stage you need to let go to allow for something new. When you do a new red impulse is born, momentum builds, and transformation occurs. And the process continues…

Color Graphics

A ll the different tints and shades are born when a color meets the polarity of light and dark. If we visualize the circle of colors with all the hues from red to yellow, green, blue and purple at the equator of the globe, and then we place white at the top and black at the bottom, a *Color Sphere* is created. This illustrates the intricate relationship between color hues, brightness and saturation.

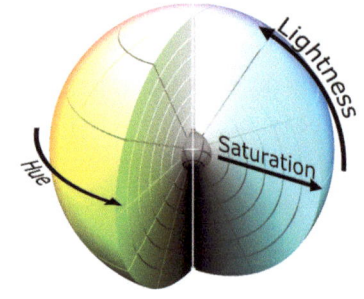

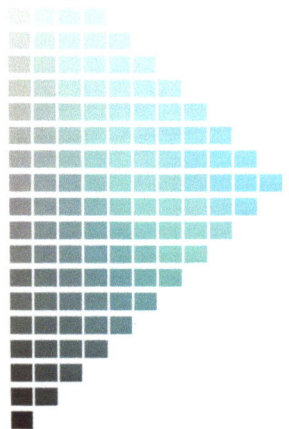

Another way of showing the same thing, while focusing on one particular color hue, is the *Color Triangle*. If we start with any color hue (at the right corner of the triangle) and move towards the left, we see how its saturation is reduced. On the left side we can see the different degrees of brightness, which changes from a high degree at the top to a low degree at the bottom. Along with these shifts the quality and meaning of a color, as well as how it affects us, changes.

Four distinct color groups, that will be further explored in *Basic Life Patterns*, can now be identified. (Note that this is merely a hint to explain the distinction between these groups. Showing the exact color nuances is not possible like this. On the one hand it is impossible to control the result after print, on the other a color nuance also depends on the surface of the colored object to a large extent.)

High saturation
A strong, bright color hue, without any interference of black or white, creates a high, intense energy that expresses the core quality of the given color hue to the fullest.

High brightness - low saturation
With a high percentage of light pastel shades are created, which changes the color quality to one of open lightness.

Low brightness - high saturation
As dark is added depth and a hint of gravity is added to the color hue.

Low brightness - low saturation
Dark colors that are also more dull (a low level of intensity) makes the color quality more grounded and stable. This also lowers the amount of emotional energy in the color hue.

Color Interpretation

C olors are a highly advanced language of energy that is best understood by a lot of experience. Practicing this language is an exercise in entering a different dimension that exists beyond any preconceived ideas about what is good or bad. We need to use our innate sensitivity, open up to how each of them feels and how we are affected by their different frequencies.

To get more acquainted with every color, while also raising your self-awareness, you can take a pause after reading about each of them and ask yourself these, or similar, questions:

- Do I like this color?
- What is my relationship to it?
- Do I dress in it regularly, rarely, or not at all?
- Have I used this color earlier in my life?
- If so, how was my life different at that time?
- Which of the shades do I prefer and why?
- What does this say about my personality?
- Could this color help me find a better balance?

Since colors can never be adequately expressed in words I have tried to keep the interpretation of each basic color down to as few words as possible. So try to read each interpretation only as a hint, or suggestion. Trust your own experience. It can be helpful to keep reminding yourself that colors are a spectrum from a warm and extrovert energy that is grounded in the outer, material world, to a more cold and introvert that is more at home in inner realities. One opens up outwards, the other inwards. One way to understand them is to relate them to different levels of life experience.

Red

Since red is the lowest frequency among the colors, it is associated with warmth as well as basic physical needs, security and survival. Physiologically it stimulates a faster heartbeat and breathing.

Red is always an impulse for action and external activity. It brings willpower and the ability to stand our ground. One of its great gifts is courage. Its specific energy helps us explore unknown places and dare new things. The color is also associated with physical strength.

If it is too much

All things become negative if they are exaggerated. Red can turn into impatience, frustration, anger and stress. Too much of it makes it difficult to relax and might burn us out. When the red energy is imbalanced it can also make us more insensitive, impatient and aggressive.

If there's a lack or blockage

Too little red energy can make us lethargic and scared of many things, so that we don't dare to take a different route in life or speak up. A lack of red energy also makes us less grounded.

Wearing the color

Red is often found in people's wardrobes, usually in sportswear. In many cultures it is a traditional color, probably because characteristics like courage and willpower are common ideals.

Different shades

<u>A strong, bright color hue</u>

Action, will, courage, strength

<u>Pastel shades</u>

Romantic love, naivety, excitement, loving trust

Dark intense colors
Passion, intense passionate love
Dark muted colors
Steadfastness, ambition, leadership, drive for material success

Orange

Orange is connected to our second chakra and relates to creativity as well as sexuality. It's an energy that makes us feel vital and enthusiastic. It can loosen up our fears and stimulate physical activity. The orange vibration is extrovert and enhances our ability to joyfully take part in social activities, to bring a sense of belonging. Friendships and intimate relationships are important. Orange can strengthen our appetite for life's pleasures, as well as for food. The good news is that it can also speed up our metabolism.

If it is too much
If the orange energy is imbalanced, it might make us wallow in the pleasures of life. We might overextend ourselves and get lost in a whirlwind of fun activities.

If there's a lack or blockage
If this energy is missing we can feel tired, worn out and stuck in a rut, with no creative sparks or sex drive whatsoever. There might be a lack of self-worth or shame around sexuality.

Wearing the color
Bright orange is a color that is rare, or even non-existent, in most people's wardrobes. Its most intense shades might be a bit too much. Darker and less saturated nuances like terracotta, or lighter like peach or salmon, is more common and easier to wear for many.

Different shades

A strong, bright color hue

Vitality, enthusiasm, life-gusto

Pastel shades

Friendly affection, a light and happy mood

Dark intense colors

Physical pleasure

Dark muted colors

Aesthetic endeavors, enjoying arts & crafts

Yellow

Yellow is the brightest color in the spectrum. We associate it with joy, spontaneity and positive expectations, which is obvious in expressions like "golden moments" or "a golden opportunity". This color also provides mental clarity and flexibility, which can inspire new ideas and originality. Yellow makes us quick-witted, provides a good sense of humor and makes us stimulating to be around. It also hints of confidence along with personal power.

If it is too much

If the yellow frequency is exaggerated it can turn into deceitfulness, cunning flattery, slander or a calculating shrewdness and cynicism. It can also lead to "butterflies in the stomach" when there are high expectations on us, or when our own expectations are high in a situation. Status, prestige and recognition might be overly important.

If there's a lack or blockage

When this energy is deficient we can be anxious and might fail to see things in a positive light. Our self-esteem might be low, so we feel insecure and don't expect much from life.

Wearing the color

Since yellow is the brightest of the colors in the spectrum, the strongest hues can be challenging to wear if you don't like to stand out in a crowd.

Different shades

A strong, bright color hue

Spontaneity, optimism, joy, originality

Pastel shades

Happy, witty, talkative, curious

Dark intense colors

Wisdom - a more embodied form of clarity and insight

Dark muted colors

Analytic, mental stability, precision

Green

Green is the balancing point between the polarized forces of red and blue, which is why it is neither active nor passive, neither extrovert nor introvert, neither material nor spiritual. Things slow down, stabilize and we are brought back to the present moment.

This brings a sense of rest that helps us recuperate, heal and gain momentum for further growth and abundance. Green is the color of the heart in the chakra system, associated with love, understanding, compassion and empathy.

If it is too much

If the green energy dominates we can overextend ourselves. We might give too much, flip into a victim role and become "green with envy". Since this color represents status quo and a degree of immobility, there can be a risk for stagnation and a reluctance to change.

If there's a lack or blockage

Too little of the green energy results in lack of stability and the ability to see things through. There is also very little mindfulness and presence. Our ability to trust others can be low and forgiveness might be difficult.

Wearing the color

Green is not one of the most common colors for clothes, even though many hues and shades are very easy to wear.

Different shades

A strong, bright color hue

Generous, loving abundance

Pastel shades

Hope and friendly sympathy

Dark intense colors

Deep compassion

Dark muted colors

Stability, material security, traditional

Turquoise

Turquoise blue is an uplifting energy that helps us observe life from a higher vantage point. We begin to reflect, which marks the first step in our search for truth. The knowledge and understanding we gain can lead to an independent personal standpoint as well as self growth.

Turquoise is connected to communication and the throat. If this area is balanced our integrity and power of self-expression develops. To talk or write about our perspective becomes more important.

If it is too much

An excessive dose of the energy can make us overly analytical and turn us into a cold, dissociated spectator, a know-it-all or a nitpicking perfectionist.

If there's a lack or blockage
Without this energy it can be difficulty to distance ourselves from the hustle-bustle of everyday life and take time to reflect upon our lives as well as life in general. A blockage can bring a lot of fear around speaking up and expressing ourselves.

Wearing the color
Turquoise is a popular color for summer clothes and the bright hues are common and easy to wear.

Different shades
A strong, bright color hue
Truth and understanding
Pastel shades
Transparent communication
Dark intense colors
Deep reflection
Dark muted colors
Critical evaluation

Blue

Our heart rate and breathing slow down with the blue energy, which helps us relax and go deeper. On this frequency we find the serious seeker with a potential for complex thinking, who gains insight through contemplation and philosophy, and focuses on self-actualization.

We also find characteristics like loyalty, sincerity and dependability. He or she can be a humble visionary dedicated to higher ideals, who wants to contribute to the development of humanity through some kind of service. Since indigo blue is an introvert color, many who feel at home here tend to be a bit shy.

If it is too much

An overemphasis can make us "feel blue" which might turn into heavy resignation or depression. We can overthink things to the point where the gap between our inner and outer reality becomes overwhelming. There is also a risk for isolation.

If there's a lack or blockage

Since blue has a calming effect on our nervous system, a lack of this energy makes it more difficult to slow down, rest, relax and turn inwards. There might also be a lack of clarity and connection to our intuition.

Wearing the color

Blue is a global favorite, easy to wear on all occasions. Since indigo blue gives us a calm, serious and trustworthy expression, a dark shade with low saturation (which means that there are a minimum of feelings involved) is prevalent among bankers, lawyers and businessmen.

Different shades

A strong, bright color hue
Tranquility, idealism, intuition, seeker
Pastel shades
Receptive, the higher abstract mind
Dark intense colors
Devotion to the mysteries of the soul
Dark muted colors
Responsible, serious, loyal, dependable

Purple

Purple represents a link to higher dimensions beyond form. Its frequency connects us with a spirituality that has nothing to do with religion, where life beyond time and space are important parts.

In tune with this realm our personal boundaries can be transcended. Inner experiences might provide us with visions, guidance as well as artistic inspiration. Because of the strong sensitivity for the subtleties of life, there can be a tendency to withdraw from the noisy everyday world.

If it is too much
Purple is also related to mental disorders and chaos, to losing touch with ordinary reality. If the purple energy is strong in us, it is extra important to do what we can to stay grounded.

If there's a lack or blockage
A difficulty to access this frequency can result in a personality that cannot relate to the more subtle realms of life, where things like spirit or higher consciousness are simply words. There can also be a lack of inspiration.

Wearing the color
Purple is a color that is quite rare in clothes. People seem to either love or hate it. Those who love it usually own several garments that they wear often, while others only dress in purple when it's in fashion. And then there are those who would never wear it.

Different shades
A strong, bright color hue
Magic ritual, sovereignty
Pastel shades
Inspiration, visions, dreams

<u>Dark intense colors</u>

Spiritual dedication and experiences

<u>Dark muted colors</u>

Translating inspiration to a tangible aesthetic expressions.

Using Colors as Tools

A s we begin to see colors – along with all their different hues, shades and tints – as expressions of energies and frequencies, a great tool to help us shape and design our personal characteristics is given to us..

Deciding what colors to wear for the day (which is usually connected to the dominant colors in our energy field at that specific time) most of us are guided by the mood we are in. A bright and happy mood equals bright colors. If we don't really want to be the center of attention we might choose grays and beiges to match our aura. Feeling depressed, or very focused and serious, darker or colder colors seem to match us better. Without self awareness we simply repeat our emotional and behavioral patterns.

When we have become aware that the colors of our clothes add vibrations to our energy field, and that we can add a color we are not used to wearing (a quality that might be unknown to us), we can begin to use our clothes as tools for inner growth. As we open up to the new color frequencies our energy field begins to shift to match that energy. Over time we become more balanced. To grow means expanding our energy field, gradually becoming more at home in larger parts of who we are.

Dynamic Blueprints

E verything – from the smallest molecule to the cycles of nature, from infinite galaxies to cosmic movements – has fundamental patterns behind them. Even the development or our own bodies, that begins with a single fertilized human egg, reflects a progression of 3D patterns. The Golden Ratio and the Fibonacci sequence are found in our DNA, all over the human body as well as in snow flakes, shells and sunflowers in the natural world. Fractal designs in coastlines, as well as the spherical shapes of planets, confirm that certain patterns and mathematical principles underlie all structures and growth processes.

The resemblance between rivers in satellite images of earth, the root system or branches of a tree and the bronchial system of the human respiratory system, is as obvious as the likeness between a human fingerprint and the growth rings of a tree. The similarities are so obvious that it can sometimes even be difficult to know what you are looking at.

None of this is a coincidence. At the most fundamental levels of life there are energy patterns that form in predetermined arrangements. These dynamic, vibrating fields can be seen as the blueprints of creation that govern all that we see and interact with – from the birth of a star to the development of a human body. Each organizing force field, or geometric shape, includes an underlying code that informs the fabric of reality. Without them our bodies, and the universe, would only consist of scattered particles. Geometric shapes thus serve as a kind of bridge between our physical existence, the laws of nature and the unseen dimensions of energy and consciousness.

> The universe cannot be understood
> unless one learns the language and letters in which it is written.
> It is written in the language of mathematics
> and its letters are triangles, circles, and other geometric figures.
> Without learning this language and these letters
> we cannot understand a single word of it
> and we keep wandering in a dark labyrinth.
> *G. Galilei*

The basic geometric shapes are found in all cultures along with a rich, ancient symbolism that has remained unchanged throughout history. In the ancient traditions of Egypt and India geometry has long been recognized as a foundational element of their cosmological and spiritual beliefs. It was referred to as Sacred Geometry – a spiritual science and a divine language of creation – that holds the secrets to manifestation as well as the control of mind and spirit. They knew that the impact of geometry reaches beyond physical shape and form, into the realms of frequency and energy, and used the different symbols as an introduction to metaphysics. Healing practices through art and architecture were also developed.

The great art traditions of mankind, from China to the North American Navajo, who perform healing rituals with the aid of geometric sand paintings, have all been attracted to the same underlying geometric structures. The simpler the shape, the stronger it expresses its message. Abstract shapes (as compared to complex objects and reproductions of things, animals or humans) take our attention away from everyday phenomena. This is something that is used in islamic art, where intricate geometric patterns are created to awaken more subtle realities, beyond the tangible world.

Along with the rational mindset of the modern paradigm, the recognition of the impact of shapes on human systems has been dismissed as super-stition. Shapes have been reduced to abstract art and technical or mathematical constructs – to static outer forms devoid of any deeper content or function.

But things are changing. The scientific community is beginning to rediscover the importance of geometry. There is a growing interest in the effect of different shapes on our health, since they seem to strengthen and balance our biofield in different ways, and thereby facilitate healing. Recent studies in the field of regenerative medicine and tissue engineer-ing opens new avenues for innovative disease treatments. A study at the University of Chicago looked at how geometry influences stem cell differentiation. They found that identical cells turned into bone cells or fat cells, depending on which of two different kinds of shapes they were exposed to. Other studies are done to look into how geometry can play a part in deactivating certain viruses.

> This natural geometry exists everywhere.
> Where there is matter, there is geometry.
> *Johannes Kepler*

All shapes that surround us affect our psyche. Even though we are not conscious of their inherent meaning, we seem to know it anyway. In numerous coaching sessions and workshops, when I have asked partici-pants to choose the shapes they prefer, I have witnessed how they pick the ones that are connected to the primary parts of their personalities. If we want to know more about a culture we can simply look at the dominant shapes that are used in architecture and design. In modern western culture straight lines, right angles, squares and rectangles are most common. The ordinary person lives in square houses, sleeps in rectangular beds and looks out through windows shaped by right angles. These are all quiet statements that our culture is bent towards more material, technical and rational ways of life.

If we look at cultures where people live in harmony with nature they use more circular or spiral shapes. The Eskimos had their igloos and the Indians their tee-pees. Below is a statement about "the white man's house" by the Indian chief Black Elk:

"It is a bad way to live, because there is no power in squares. Everything the Power of the World does is done in a circle. The sky is round, and I have heard that the earth is round like a ball, and so are all the stars. The wind, in its greatest power, whirls. Birds make their nests in circles, for theirs is the same religion as ours. The sun comes forth and goes down again in a circle. The moon does the same, and both are round. Even the seasons form a great circle in their changing, and always come back again to where they were. The life of a man is a circle from childhood to childhood, and so it is in everything where power moves. Our tepees were round like the nests of birds, and these were always set in a circle, the nation's hoop, a nest of many nests, where the Great Spirit meant for us to hatch our children. But the white man has put us in these square houses. Our power is gone and we are a dying people…"

Sacred Geometry tells us about the different qualities of shapes. Early on, as I pondered their significance, I was deeply intrigued. Colors and shapes both express different qualities, and both had something to do with energy and vibrations. So what was the difference? How could I make a clear distinction between them? After immersing myself in a lot of deep contemplation, along with contemporary studies and mystical traditions, I came to this conclusion:

There is an interdependent relationship between colors and shapes, or life force and structure. When they merge the expression of both is refined. Since the flow of energy, that we interpret as colors, is without boundaries it needs to be contained by a geometric shape that "holds the space" and also directs it towards a certain development. A shape depends on colors to give it a content of feelings and life experience.

Since clothes are our focus in this book, the connection to shapes can be related either to the overall shape of a garment (which is more difficult to carry out) or to fabric patterns. I have found it most interesting to focus on patterns for fabrics, since this is where shapes can be used in a really obvious and clear way. It does limit us to 2-dimensional shapes, though.

Geometric shapes offer a set of codes that can be useful in our process of growth. Like colors they sneak past our logical mind and tell us, in a symbolic language, how life force is shaped and directed. There is also a progressive sequence that shows us something about an overall human development.

Maybe the most important thing is that our recognition of shapes is a way to reclaim our relationship to an original language, based on a deeper experience than logical thinking. So let's start to become more conscious of their meaning, as well as how they affect us, by taking a closer look at the most common basic shapes.

A Point of Focus

"In the beginning there was nothing. And then there was light." Similar ways of expressing the same thing can be found in many creation myths. The evolution of shapes actually follows a similar story, that seems to tell us about an overall development.

A point of consciousness appears. This marks the beginning of space-time, the starting point of an evolutionary cycle. Even though the point has no outside or inside, and doesn't exist as a shape of its own, it represents the origin and potential of everything manifested. It can be seen as a seed, with an inherent longing to express all that it is, that eventually searches for its way back to nothingness.

The point is often referred to as the zero-dimensional point, singularity or source of divine unity. The point thus represents a gateway to higher planes beyond time and space. It is the white as well as the black hole in space, where worlds are born as well as extinguished.

Seen from a human standpoint a point helps us be still and focus our energy. This ability, which is often practiced through meditation, is needed to go deeper and experience higher states of being.

The Circle of Wholeness

A circle (often with a point at its center) shows us a new stage in the process of evolution. There is a radiating or spiraling movement as the singular focus of the point expands outwards to create a circle. It is like a Big Bang, materializing a container for a world that can hold all possibilities.

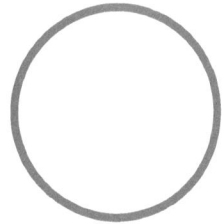

The circle is one of our oldest symbols. We find it everywhere in nature; the annual rings of a tree, the concentric ripples on water, the orbits of planets and the gradual change of seasons. We honor the circular nature of life as we embrace the fluidity of existence. We "come full circle" after going through a cycle of development or completing a certain stage of life.

A plain circle represents a container for entirety, for all that is, all that we are. Since a circle has no beginning and no end, it is a timeless symbol for continuity, wholeness and oneness that connect us across time and space. In the circle we are all equal. No one is in front of us, behind us, above or below us. All life, all potential and all possibilities are included, resting in an eternal now. Among the basic shapes a circle is the only one that has rounded edges and is usually referred to as feminine.

Circles have been used for millennia in sacred rituals for the purpose of inner connection and healing. From a psychological point of view it symbolizes psychic wholeness, the inner space where we can be nurtured and healed. It also represents a state of complete openness and receptivity. Circles help us reach this open space where the totality of what is there in the moment is acknowledged and accepted. This state of mind helps us gain insight as well as inspiration.

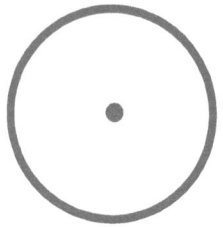 A circle with a central point is often called a Mandala, and drawing one is a method used to explore the psyche – a practice that can indicate a new beginning or mark some kind of completion. It is also an art form where an array of symbols, shapes and forms emanate from the center.

Our eyes contain a natural mandala and are often called "The Window of the Soul". When you look into someone's eyes the pupil seems to hold some mysterious power.

The mandala is an archetypal image
whose occurrence is attested throughout the ages.
This circular image represents the wholeness of the Self
or, to put it in mythic terms, divinity incarnate in man.
Carl Gustav Jung

The spiral is another ancient symbol, closely connected to the circle. Its outward movement represents creation or manifestation, while the winding journey inwards is the one we must make to truly know ourselves. A return to center always reveals something new about life and who we are. As we  move outwards again, we do so with increased insight and wisdom.

Curves and wavy lines are born out of this spiraling movement. They generate energy and increase flexibility.

The Dividing Line

From the point at the center of the circle there is now a movement in two opposite directions. In this process all that existed as potential in the circle of wholeness is split up. Duality is created and difference appears as we reach the first dimension of the line. Light is separated from darkness, male from female, warm from cold and good from bad.

As we leave the state of wholeness our awareness is divided into conscious and unconscious. We become identified with certain traits, while others fall into oblivion. Through this division a kind of mirror is created for us, where things we can no longer see in ourselves are reflected through others. This split into polarities starts a process searching for who we really are. It also creates a feeling of separation and in many languages there is a connection between two and doubt. Even though this state of mind can be a potential conflict, it is also a creative tension.

Along with this experience of separation we are metaphorically cast out of paradise, out of blissful unity. We realize that we are different. But this state is a prerequisite for our intellect. In order to think and see things in perspective, we must be able to separate things and occurrences from each other.

This development is reflected in human consciousness when an infant learns to separate between itself and its mother. Eventually it also learns the difference between boy and girl, and becomes more and more objective, more able to separate, more prone to put itself outside of the experience in a situation.

Lines help us discern, analyze and be objective. A line also marks a boundary. When it is horizontal it is calm and passive, while a vertical line is more confronting and seems to demand something from us.

Triangle Dynamics

A triangle symbolizes a process that is born out of the state of duality and polarization. The tension between opposite poles marks the starting point for a creative process and a movement from a state of conflict towards a higher synthesis and unity.
The lines that went outwards in opposite directions are now drawn towards a common goal, a third point. From this overall view we realize that polarity was the necessary driver to ignite this development to a more complex and advanced state of mind.

A triangle, or a corner with an acute angle (less than 90 degrees), always represents a state of dynamic tension that needs an outlet. This leads to a development where the energy is directed in a specific direction to release tension. A creative process often begins with some kind of frustration or a state of conflict. If we can raise above this state of mind, embrace polarities and allow them to interact, new ideas can be born.

In our human evolution this state can be represented by puberty, when tension as well as attraction between the sexes is awakened. In the union of man and woman there is a potential for a child (something new) to be born, which is also an expression of the process behind this shape.

Triangles direct our energy towards an intention. They strengthen the creative process and remind our unconscious mind of the possibility for higher complexity.

The Stable Square

The square symbolizes manifestation – the creation or appearance of matter – and thus a physical dimension where things are set in a firm, concrete form. In this mindset our primary drive is a need for stability, for that which can be managed, dependable and controlled. A square thus helps us to be grounded and realistic, with an ability to see what is practically viable within a given frame. Life experience is focused in a set time and space, where we enjoy our material creations. In its extreme nothing exists outside of these borders. The square thus also represents the psychological stage where we are limited within the set form of our conditioned personality.

A square consists of right angles of 90 degrees. This is an unrelenting angle that represents something immovable and thus stable. Energy is controlled within certain limits.

The square is the total opposite of the circle. But the two are often depicted together, either as a square inside a circle or a circle within a

173

square. This represents the constant interaction between unlimited possibilities (circle), and manifestation (square). It can also show a state of full embodiment, where our Soul merges with our physical identity.

Because of its right angles the symbol of the cross is closely related to the square. It does have a slightly different meaning, though. The cross has existed as a symbol for a very long time and was initially a symbol of reproduction, pointing to the separation, as well as the union, between male and female that generated new life. In mathematics we use the plus sign when we add up two units.

With the crucifixion of Christ the cross also became a symbol for suffering and death. Since its lines accentuate separation on a vertical level (the right from the left parts of us) as well as a horizontal (the spiritual from the material), we can understand how this limits consciousness. Stuck in this state we are symbolically "nailed to the cross" and experience separation and suffering.

Expansion of Consciousness

While the circle, line, triangle and square are closely related to certain personality types, they also describe the developmental stages that can be represented by the four basic elements – water, air, fire and earth. As you read about these basic shapes you might have felt more drawn to some of them, which helps you gain insights about your personality. The four basic elements need to be balanced before we move on towards higher stages of inner growth. In the chapter called *Basic Life Patterns* we will look at this more closely.

The evolution of shapes tells us about how consciousness expands to add new dimensions and increasingly complex realities. Each level helps us perceive things differently and changes our perspective of what we call reality. As we move on through the evolution of form it becomes obvious that the shapes that represent this further development all have obtuse angles (more than 90 degrees) in their outer form that gradually widen. This moves us towards increasing openness and ease (as opposed to tension with acute angles). The shapes also begin to look more and more like a circle. It is as if we, when we move beyond the stage represented by the square, are set on a journey back to wholeness (represented by the circle).

What is interesting to note is that inside of these shapes there are stars with a growing number of arms, whose angles become increasingly acute. It is as if the tension and drive of acute angles is now moved to an inner level, towards inner growth.

The shapes described in the following chapters are rarely seen in fabric patterns. Since the specific stages of evolution they describe are not yet very common in Western culture, this makes perfect sense.

Pentagram

The pentagram tells us about the journey from a conditioned personality to becoming an individual – one who is not divided. It represents the expansion of awareness to a conscious and self-aware human, a state where we have gained insight about a higher reality where everything is interconnected. We rediscover the Self.

The five-pointed star inside the pentagram can be seen as an image of man, with the legs down, the arms outwards and the head at the top. This top represents the higher consciousness that raises man above the four basic stages of evolution. The higher mind (sometimes referred to as the element of ether) rules over matter. We consciously raise ourselves above concrete reality and become co-creators of life. When the penta-gram is depicted with the top down it symbolizes a destructive process, where subjective desires (instead of higher consciousness) rules the individual.

Images or patterns with pentagrams subconsciously reminds us of the process of becoming an individual. It helps us open up to balance the basic elements in our psyche, relate to our personality more objectively and begin to identify with the Self.

Hexagram

Inherent in the shape called a hexagram is the figure of two interpenetrating equilateral triangles, one pointing upwards and the other downwards. This symbolism is central to the developmental phase, since it represents the union of the polarities of 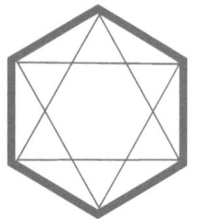 masculine and feminine, body and soul, spirit and matter, thus forming a new archetypal whole. We become the embodiment of our soul and align with our true purpose and passion on Earth.

The hexagram is a shape that occurs throughout nature. The best-known is the bees' honeycomb where the precision is so astonishing that many see it as a manifestation of divine harmony in nature. Another hexagonal form is snowflakes which, despite the infinite number of unique variations, always consists of this six-fold symmetry. The crystals of many gems and minerals are also hexagonal.

In Sacred Geometry this shape is also called The Merkaba (Mer-Ka-Bah means light-spirit-body) and is said to be a tool that can be used to transcend to higher dimensions.

The hexagram assists us in the process of integrating our innermost polarity – that of feminine and masculine aspects.

Heptagram

Through the developmental process described in the hexagram, we became the embodiment of our soul. The following stage of development is defined by the Heptagram – a sacred symbol of a sevenfold manifestation from one indivisible center.

We find its expression in the seven properties of matter. Exactly what these seven are is a bit unclear, but it is interesting to note that sounds, colors, days etc, are grouped in sevens. There are also seven "sources of magic": north, south, east, west, above, below, and within. As a magical number, seven is considered a symbol of eternity. In the Kabbalah (a school of thought in Jewish mysticism) seven has always been the number of completion.

In theory we could go on to draw a shape that has 8 corners. If we did an Octagram would follow. There are certainly more dimensions than the ones mentioned, so we definitely could. But in this context it has no relevance. The further we would move along, the more difficult it would be for us to relate to it as a state of development. Since the Heptagram represents the highest stage of needs mentioned in earlier chapters, it makes sense to stop here.

You have probably noticed already that there is a correlation between many of these shapes and the developmental processes described in the section *A Set of Needs*. I have chosen to keep them apart, since I know that mixing different systems is never a good idea. This part of the book is also more focused on visuals, created as an entry point into a new approach to the design of clothes and fabrics patterns. So let's move our focus back to clothes and look at ways to use this knowledge.

Impact on Repeat

P atterns exist all around us. The natural world speaks in patterns and we find them everywhere – on flowers, insects and shells. Others are created by human hands, like the ones for interior design or fabrics used for clothes. So are these simply made to make surfaces more pleasing to the eye, or is there any deeper purpose behind these patterns?

After our closer look at the different languages of colors and shapes, as well as how these are related to human consciousness, the answer to this question is quite obvious. Through patterns there is a constant expression of the qualities that make our inner patterns of behavior and experience visible. The crux of the matter is that we seem to have forgotten about the impact of visual patterns, which keeps this intriguing subject unrecognized.

We began to decorate our bodies through different methods of permanent tattooing early on in human history. Even though the symbolism varied, this was practiced by many cultures across the globe. It would be logical to assume that these markings were later transferred onto body covering hides and, over time, to fabrics for clothes.

Even though nobody knows for sure what gave rise to our need to decorate ourselves, what we *do* understand is that it wasn't a practical need. Most probably it wasn't simply regarded as a beautiful decoration either. One of the theories as to why the first decorative patterns were created, is that they had magical significance and symbolized different forces. Drawing them on the skin, a hide or piece of cloth, was a way of evoking their power. To cover the body with different shapes and symbols is believed to have been a practice of embodying magical forces in order to empower or protect the wearer.

The ancient Greeks, who had a developed sense of rhythm and symmetry, used the term *kosmos* with the double meaning of decoration and cosmic order. One who had similar thoughts was Gottfried Semper, a German architect and art expert who lived in the second half of the 19th century. According to him decoration was really a search for harmony in the laws of nature and a response to a universal order. This approach has remained in the traditional Japanese perspective of beauty. In his book *The Unknown Craftsman*, Soetsu Yanagi states that the making of patterns involves a strict observance of principles. Patterns represent order which means numbers or laws. Good patterns cannot be made without observance of these laws.

According to other Eastern traditions the ceremonial pictures created for meditation and visualization called *thankas* affect our thinking. They are painted or embroidered on cloth according to traditional geometric patterns, where certain color combinations represent different aspects of our mind. What stands out is that it is the observer's experience of the thanka that is important, not the art itself. In her book *Holy, Healing Pictures* Gun Maij Aronsson writes about these thankas: "The quality of a picture – its energetic content – has a great effect on the observer. Colors and shapes send out radiation and transmit vibrations on different frequencies. The invisible elements behind the pictures – the idea, the power and the technique, as well as the combination of patterns and colors – create an effect on our way of thinking as well as on how we act and express ourselves."

In sacred and meditative art it is important to avoid all personification. All that is nonessential is taken away to make the experience more impactful. If we see a pattern with horses, flowers or some object from everyday life, we might have an association to a personal experience. But a simple shape affects, and connects us to, deeper levels of our being. Fabric patterns for clothes, along with all decorative art, can thus reinforce certain energies. If the patterns we create, and surround ourselves with, are made with awareness of their effects they can bring inner balance and healing.

> Since pattern is a portrayal of the intuitively perceived essence
> all non-essentials must be stripped away.
> Good patterns are simple;
> if they are cluttered they are not yet patterns.
> *Soetsu Yanagi*

The universal language of decorative patterns is rich. Just like a song, a dance or a painting it can be expressive, dramatic and colorful, or convey a discreet regularity. It can be full of detail or very simple and strict. It can be filled with tension and contrast or express calm, resting movements.

Compared to patterns on other products, like wall-paper, shower curtains or gift wrappings, a pattern on a piece of cloth has an even greater possibility of expressing all the different qualities inherent in a human being. Through the different techniques of weaving, embroidery, knitting or printing, the expression can be refined. If we add the whole variety of textile materials that express different qualities – like soft or sturdy, flexible or firm, light or heavy, flat or heavily structured, shiny or dull – it further enriches the expression of the fabric pattern.

There is another very important difference between visual patterns in general and those on clothes. A notebook cover, or curtains with a decorative pattern, is something outside of us. They don't become part of ourselves the way clothes do. When we wear a piece of cloth with patterns close to our physical body, it enhances our experience of its inner quality. Its colors and shapes become part of our biofield and thus affects the way we perceive ourselves and the world around us.

We are flooded with images of clothes, designed objects and interior decoration on a daily basis. Depending on fashion trends there can either be a big supply of fabrics with patterns or hardly any at all. Sometimes wildly flowered patterns in bright colors are trendy and sometimes everybody wants the strictly graphic ones in grey. The ones that are always available are the checked and striped patterns, since they so thoroughly express the dominant state of mind in contemporary Western culture.

A hundred years ago a clothing style or interior design could remain in fashion for decades. Trends began to change more rapidly during the 1960's and 70's. Today they change even faster. There is also focus on creating a personal clothing style and we are more free to choose and combine clothes the way we want. But how free are we really? Since we are always drawn towards styles and patterns that express the qualities of our personality, we are more or less conditioned to pick out the garments we do. It's an subconscious choice. But as we reach the point where we become interested in personal growth it becomes a conscious process. We begin to ask ourselves questions like:

- Why do I always prefer the checked patterns?
- What quality in me do they represent?
- Do I really need to surround myself with squares?
- Is there some other quality that needs to be strengthened?
- How would that pattern look?

When this shift occurs fabric patterns become great tools that provide pleasurable contributions to inner growth.

A field of knowledge that is comparable to the balancing and healing effect of fabric patterns is the ancient Chinese practice of *Feng Shui*, where colors, patterns and objects are used to balance our home environment. *Functional Food* is a similar concept that originated in Japan in the 1980s, when the country was faced with escalating healthcare costs. A regulatory system to approve certain foods with documented benefits was initiated in an effort to improve the health of the general population. Functional Foods is usually the basics that we already have in our homes. To use them as beneficial agents we just need awareness about their specific effects. Textile patterns for clothes are also something basic and already present in our homes that can be used for beneficial purposes.

Basic Life Patterns

E ven though there are quite a lot of basic fabric patterns where we can easily identify the colors and shapes, most fabric patterns are a confusing mix of qualities. To have the strongest effect the colors and shapes need to be as pure and refined as possible.

A few things are vital if we want to use patterns as tools for balancing and integrating purposes. First of all we need an intention. Some self awareness is also essential. We can then proceed to ask ourselves if we need to strengthen a certain energy or if there are parts that need to be integrated. With some knowledge about different colors and shapes we can begin to look for clothes with the fabric patterns needed.

There is a close relationship between invisible human life patterns and visible decorative patterns. One way of describing our most common behavior patterns is to relate them to the basic elements. In the chapter *The Wisdom of the Pyramid* we learned about the need to balance these elements to find better stability before we move on to the next stage of development. The first step in beginning to make our "psychological ground" more steady is thus to balance these four. If one of them is weak, or if we have no connection to it at all, it needs to be strengthened and integrated.

A good place to begin our journey of becoming more conscious when we choose clothes with patterns, or if we design patterns ourselves, is to get more acquainted with these basic elements and what they are about.

Looking more closely at the descriptions below of each one of them will also help you recognize your own most prominent elements as well the ones that are most difficult for you to relate to.

WATER - heavy and flexible
The unconscious. Our instinctive emotional life.
Water floats around obstacles and has very little resistance. With a good connection to this element we tend to be quite flexible and easily influenced by the outer world. Since we are also receptive, and have a strong connection to our sensitive and vulnerable sides, we can easily become overwhelmed and might crave alone time regularly.

In a similar way that water penetrates the earth, this element tends to go in depth, to focus on the inner life of feelings, dreams and symbols. A strong connection to water gives us the ability to intuit the more subtle levels of life, that might bring a deep inner knowing without any specific source. This intuitive knowing can be difficult to express in words and is most easily expressed through art, poetry or music. The heaviness of the element can also make us feel low, or even depressed, at times.
Pattern: Movement and depth.
Shapes: Patterns based on circles, spirals or curves.
Colors: Deep and intense colors add emotional depth (low brightness/ high saturation).

AIR - light and flexible
Interpersonal connections. Ideas.
This invisible element blows fresh air into life as it whirls around and creates movement. The element is closely tied to different kinds of relationships between people – from the close intimate ones to larger social groups – and the exchange of thoughts, ideas or information during these interactions. Strongly influenced by air we are socially gifted, with an ability to understand a large variety of perspectives, as well as seeing things objectively. We like to be engaged in different projects, built on

creative and future oriented concepts.

The element of air strengthens our logical ability. It helps us discern, analyze and be objective, to understand complexity and larger contexts. The ability to be openminded, mentally quick and flexible makes it easy for us to see things clearly and to handle information effectively.

A tendency to be "up in the air" might separate us from our feelings (water), as well as the body and practical daily life (earth).

Pattern: Light movement.

Shapes: Patterns built on lines.

Colors: Pastel shades (high brightness/low saturation) make the patterns more light and open.

FIRE - light and firm

Our individuality.

A fire is dynamic and expansive. This element represents our human life force. Strongly identified with it we are convinced that life is full of meaning. We often have a good measure of self-reliance that springs from knowing our own unique value. Full of enthusiasm we can inspire and motivate others – to lead as well as teach. The element also makes us dynamic, action driven and goal oriented. Our strong will, along with a firm and straightforward way of communicating and operating, is used to make things happen in the world. With the fiery element strongly prevalent warmth, affection and love is shown openly. Our expression can be intense and dramatic with emotions like joy, passion as well as anger.

Without a good balance to the other elements all this determination and drive might lead to burnout, and we tend to be a bit insensitive to other people's feelings. To be passive and acknowledge feelings like sorrow or resignation can also be difficult.

Pattern: A dynamic expression.

Shapes: Patterns with triangular shapes.

Colors: Strong, bright colors (high saturation) creates an intense energy.

EARTH - heavy and firm
The material reality. Stability.
Earth is stable. It keeps our feet firmly planted on the ground, gives us a large dose of common sense and helps us see things "the way they are". Things like function, order and security motivate us to stick to things that are known and tested. Identified with this element traditions are important to us. We also tend to be loyal, dependable and responsible. If we have promised to do something it will get done, no matter what.

With an earthy personality our attempts to satisfy basic needs in the concrete world are in focus, and our interests might be quite physical and practical. Earth helps us be realistic, see what is practically viable and carry things through. When we want to change something we do it through planning, a practical and structured execution and a good dose of patience.

If this element is imbalanced there can be an exaggerated need for stability, which makes flexibility difficult and change impossible. If too weak it can be difficult for us to be organized.
Pattern: Disciplined and well structured.
Shapes: Squares and rectangles. Right angles.
Colors: Dark, warm, more muted colors (low brightness/low saturation) enhances stability.

Another division can be added to these four types. In the chapter *Three Faces of Color* we looked at the colors in three phases: red, green and blue.

RED   The first manifestation of the element's inherent quality.
             A bold and daring impulse for action to create, or start,
             something new.

GREEN   We stabilize and consolidate what was created.
             Perseverance and resilience.

BLUE   We study, adapt and transform that which was created and consolidated.
Flexibility and change.

This division of colors helps us understand and clarify the three developmental stages of each element, i.e. how the inherent quality of the element can express itself in different ways. It gives us a more refined tool to direct a pattern towards a specific stage of a process.

Four elements, divided into three stages each, create 12 variations, or life patterns. Interesting enough these correspond to the 12 astrological signs, which describe the fundamental archetypes inherent in all of us.

An important note here is that even though our astrological sun sign is usually an obvious part of our personality, it is not as simple as that. Our personal horoscope, which is based on the exact time and place of our birth, gives us a unique combination of several planets placed in different signs and houses. This means that we all have a unique mix of elements. While some are visible and well balanced in our personality, others might be blocked or unknown to us. So if you identify with some patterns more than others that is no coincidence.

Three stages of the element WATER
Red water (Cancer)
An impulse to meet the outside world on an emotional level.
Reaching out to care for others and provide emotional support.
Green water (Scorpio)
Emotions are held back to be experienced and explored.
Holding on to some reliable psychological model to understand our inner life.
Blue water (Pisces)
Delving into deep emotional processes, where ego boundaries are dissolved and transformed.
Gaining access to the collective subconscious to intuit deeper realities.

Three stages of the element AIR

Red air (Libra)

Creative ideas. Outward action to communicate and interact.

Seeking out and exploring the relationship between self and the other.

Green air (Aquarius)

Using abstract intellect to understand relationships in larger social groups.

Holding on to different models of understanding.

Blue air (Gemini)

Curiosity of people and ideas.

Mental flexibility and quick changes of perspectives.

Three stages of the element FIRE

Red fire (Aries)

Actions to express our will.

Courage to explore and conquer new frontiers.

Green fire (Leo)

Self-confidence, dignity and self-respect.

A solid platform for self-fulfillment.

Blue fire (Sagittarius)

Freedom, expansion and wisdom.

Transforming the world according to our own understanding.

Three stages of the element EARTH

Red earth (Capricorn)

An impulse to organize, build and produce things in physical reality.

Independent and enterprising.

Green earth (Taurus)
Stabilizes that which was created, perseverance to see things through and make them durable.
Conservative. Holds on to, as well as enjoys, the material world.
Blue earth (Virgo)
Using the knowledge of our material world to make things more efficient.
Material transformation and change.

Since the elements, and their different stages of development, can also be combined in various ways to enhance integration, there are endless ways to create patterns that help us towards inner balance and wholeness. We will most certainly see more advanced ways of creating such patterns in the future. Using patterns to balance the basic building blocks of identity is a good way to start.

Our Inner Climate

Melting ice. Raging wildfires. Drought and floods. Tornados, land slides and extreme temperatures. We're in the midst of a climate crisis where the natural elements seem totally out of balance. Even if many of us do what we can to act responsibly, it is easy to feel as if there is no hope when huge corporations continue to focus primarily on financial gain. But there is something each one of us can do.

Even though we might believe that we can separate ourselves from it all, this is simply not possible. We are intimately intertwined with each other as well as our planet and all natural forces. The natural world is like a huge mirror that reflects our inner collective climate. So instead of fearing natural disasters, we can swing our magnifying glass around 180 degrees and take a serious look at our own inner climate.

Go inside and try to get a an image, or an intuition, of the state of your inner landscape. Is it too dry or moist, too hot or cold? Too windy? Are natural forces held back or released in uncontrollable ways? Is your life filled with extreme polarities and conflict? Are you stressed out? Do you overuse your mental capacity? How grounded are you? Have you put your career before your emotional well-being? Have you lost the spark of passion due to over-emphasis on the practical things in life? Do you carry around toxic thoughts and feelings? This will all be re-created in the world around us.

Our natural world is telling us
that inner balance has been lost.
And we are all partly responsible.

Once you figure out which elements are weak or over-emphasized, the fabric patterns of garments are excellent tools to help rebalance these natural forces. When in balance (on an outer as well as inner level) the elements of water, air, fire, earth and ether interact and balance each other in an intricate dance, where neither water nor soil, heat nor cold, dominate. So own your part of our collective climate crisis and use available tools to help you.

Fractal Patterns

The design of ordinary patterns usually follow a strict formula. A given shape, in an exact size, is repeated horizontally and vertically with a few possible and predictable variations. Even though this is in part due to the textile printing process, I believe it is also connected to the human mindsets that are based on The Old Story, where reality is seen as something predictable, where change can be planned in linear ways.

So what will happen to the patterns we surround ourselves with when we open up to perceive a larger reality that is not linear and static? Most certainly we will see different kinds of decorative patterns.

Basic geometry is important in its own way, but it is not a good way to describe life's complexity and unpredictability. Like nature life is not bound by any specific size or scale and thus cannot be seen through simple linear formulas. A better way to visualize how minute shifts result in huge and unexpected changes are fractals – the geometry of chaos.

A Fractal is a pattern that repeats endlessly.
Every part of it, regardless of how we zoom in or out
looks very similar to the whole image.

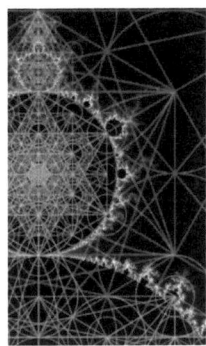

Fractal patterns are born out of a different kind of approach and transformation, some more predictable than others. We can recognize these patterns when the similarity of a small detail of, let's say, a fern and its entire leaf is obvious, or when we can zoom in endlessly while the same patterns keeps appearing. In Mandelbrot fractals there is a seemingly endless diversity of patterns where new shapes appear and disappear. It reminds us of a journey through an endless universe of colors and morphing shapes.

Dressing Archetypes

E very garment tells a unique story. A clothing style is thus like a composed story with an intricate plot. Through its many inter-related parts and layers, consisting of colors, shapes, patterns, fabric types, styles and different kinds of garments, it tells the story of an identity.

Over time it changes. Inspired by others, or simply following our own intuitive hunches, we add fragments, exchange a color for another, try out a different fit or fabric pattern. But this complex story is full of more or less hidden messages, which makes it difficult to analyze or fully understand it.

Most of us have experimented with a few different clothing styles throughout our lives, especially in our teenage years when we were quite impressionable and still a bit uncertain about our identity. Each time we entered a new phase of our lives, like starting college, becoming a parent or beginning a new job, different parts of us were activated which affec-ted how we chose to dress. Eventually we landed in a style we felt com-fortable with, which also meant that our personality became more set in a specific form. We have some variations for different types of events in our wardrobes, but our basic style is more or less the same.

So does this story, that we step into every morning, have any value besides describing our overall personality? Maybe you recall playing games as a kid where you dressed up in different outfits? You really felt changed as you did and it was so fun to pretend you were that other person. Different ways of behaving and expressing ourselves seemed to come naturally. An actor who puts on a costume experiences something similar. Different clothing styles – like the romantic, sporty, formal, laid back and more – help us identify with various attitudes, as well as ways of being and relating in the world.

The various personal ways to dress in a certain style can embody several basic elements, the inherent parts of a more complex character.

Different clothing styles can be compared to archetypes – universal energy patterns that embody specific qualities. Our personalities are predisposed for a set of archetypes that shape our experience, our behavior as well as reactions. They affect our work and our relationships, decide if we are emotionally intense and intellectually sharp or not, rule our physical activity and aesthetic sense, our longings, our perception of time and much, much more.

Even though we all recognize these archetypes, they reside on such deep subconscious levels that they cannot be explained rationally. This is why the knowledge of these individualized characteristics were passed on through worn stories, like clothes and costumes, or narrated in the form of myths and fairy tales. The Greek and Roman gods and goddesses are studies of their complexity. They tell us about the specific challenges, development as well as the fate of different archetypes.

> Until you make the unconscious conscious
> it will direct your life and you will call it fate.
> C. G. Jung

If a specific archetype is unconscious (as is the case for many of us) we can be pulled into continuous loops of troublesome situations and relationships. They can drive us and basically determine our fate. The more aware we can become of these archetypal influences, and form a conscious relationship to them, the more agency and control we have over our own lives.

As kids we got to meet many archetypes through fairy tales. In *Briar-Rose*, or *Sleeping Beauty*, we learned what happens when we don't acknowledge and honor them all.

... At the christening of a king and queen's long-wished-for daughter, only twelve of the thirteen fairies in the country were invited to be her godmothers, since they only had twelve golden plates. As the feast came to an end the fairies bestowed their magic gifts upon the baby: one gave her virtue, another beauty, a third riches and so on, with everything in the world that one can wish for.

When eleven of them had made their promises the thirteenth fairy suddenly came in. She wished to avenge herself for not having been invited and without greeting, or even looking at anyone, she cried with a loud voice: "The King's daughter shall in her fifteenth year prick herself with a spindle and fall down dead."

The last fairy had yet to give her gift and used it to partially reverse the wicked fairy's curse, proclaiming that the princess would instead fall into a deep sleep for a hundred years and be awoken by a king's son ...

There are several interesting layers to this story, which are eerily relevant to our time. The cross-cultural feminine archetypes form the different facets of the Feminine *as a whole*. (The same goes for masculine archetypes.) Each embodies unique qualities and behavior patterns. But, as we have seen in earlier chapters of this book, certain feminine archetypes are culturally disowned, like the one that expresses the so called "dark" face of the Feminine. In *Sleeping Beauty* this is hinted at since the king (the patriarch) only has twelve golden plates. (There are twelve solar (gold) and thirteen lunar (silver) months in a year.) He uses a solar (masculine) measure which causes problems for the budding feminine, who is stricken by a terrible fate. The exact same thing happens culturally, as well as in our individual psyche. The energy of the archetypes we judge, disown and refuse to acknowledge, tend to become distorted and wreak havoc in our lives.

As we discussed earlier, the reason for a part to be disowned can depend on how we were conditioned, how different roles were distributed in our family unit, or the values of the culture we grew up in. The result is the same – the archetype is repressed. But an archetype can never disappear. It lives on in our subconscious, patiently waiting to be rediscovered and included in our lives, while sending hints about their presence through outer conflict or drama.

Jean Shinoda Bolen is a psychiatrist and Jungian analyst who has written many books about the archetypal psychology of women and men. In *Goddesses in Everywomen* and *Gods in Everyman* she uses seven goddesses and eight gods from the Greek pantheon to describe the most common feminine and masculine archetypal patterns. There are others, more or less powerful, that are not among those mentioned in her book, but I believe she has found the ones that prevail in contemporary Western society and account for the major differences between women as well as between men. It's a huge subject though, so it is not possible to cover it in this book. But I recommend these, or similar, books to anyone who is interested in deepening their understanding of the most common archetypes.

Archetypes are truly a doorway to self-awareness and inner growth. It isn't that we need to activate every known archetype. The essential thing is to figure out if any are disowned so that we can learn to accept and appreciate them.

Different clothing styles can activate archetypes. Strongly identified with a certain style, and thus a specific archetype (or combinations of a few), we are probably also quite set in specific behavior patterns and an outlook on life. This in turn determines how we perceive reality and certain outcomes become more or less predetermined. It doesn't require a long stretch of our imagination to compare this to the fate of the various gods and goddesses.

Since we can use the dress-up game to experience, develop and embody them, clothing styles turn into great tools. Trying to perceive the archetypes behind certain clothing styles also helps us look at our lives from a deeper perspective than our ordinary day-to-day experience. Through them the mythic dimension of life becomes apparent.

Exploring archetypes through clothes is a handy tool to use when we are in the stage of balancing and integrating parts of our conditioned personality. As we come closer to a state of wholeness, and begin to identify with the Self, we move beyond the archetypal realm.

Tweaking our Clothing Style

A rchetypes are complex. Just like you and me they are composed of many parts. Translating them to clothing styles is thus a tricky task, even though we can get a sense of their different characters when they are described. I mean, how would you dress a magician or a trickster archetype? We could definitely use our imagination to create something that would be fitting, but would it help the person who simply wants to use their clothes to become more whole? I don't believe it would.

If we instead approach clothing styles from the perspective of common human characteristics, it is easier to relate to them. Most of us know how to dress someone to make their expression more soft, strict, innovative, active, vulnerable, laid-back, traditional, edgy or organized. We also see the repeated expression of these in endless variations in clothing stores, through styles we call romantic, basic, creative, professional, practical, sensual, bohemian or sporty.

To simply recognize what clothing styles we like, dislike or avoid helps us become more aware of our strengths as well as weaknesses. It brings us clues about styles we could use to assist us on our path towards balance and integration. It might take some introspection to understand these inner dynamics, but as the qualities we need to develop become clearer we can begin to tweak our clothing style. We don't have to go all the way, simply include a touch of the style. See how it makes us feel and act. Turn up or down the volume.

Let me share some examples from my personal experience to shed light on possible ways to tweak our clothing style.

- A formal, more professional style has always been the one furthest away from what I have identified with. I even had a tendency to look down on characteristics like being strict, traditional and overly rational. This is, of course, only a reflection of an imbalance within myself. Since I can definitely see and appreciate the values of those traits, they are not disowned, though. To find a better balance I have often mixed a tailored jacket with a more feminine or creative style. I always loved the result of blending these traits that have so little in common.

- For long periods of my life jeans were a dominant garment in my wardrobe and a natural part of my ordinary outfit. But as I began to understand how the rough surface of the fabric was related to a sturdy and rough 2nd skin, I became intrigued by how sensitivity and vulnerability were missing in that style. For a time I totally ruled out jeans, while replacing them with trousers in softer fabrics, or skirts. Nowadays I only wear jeans on occasion, for practical reasons.

- I was definitely conditioned to overvalue masculine qualities. Even though my clothing style was creative and flexible, I wasn't a "skirt and dress" kind of woman when I was younger. Oversized men's shirts with pants were my favorite. Eventually I had some powerful insights into how my feminine side had been shoved aside and began integrating skirts and dresses that agreed with my basic style. How to express the true feminine, beyond patriarchal ideals, is still a quest that intrigues and keeps inspiring me.

- The most disowned part of my psyche first showed up as a malevolent witch, while practicing the method called Voice Dialogue.

200

(Parts that are disowned tend to become twisted or demonized.) As I began to understand and appreciate this timeless feminine archetype, she slowly transformed into a true ally. Her powerful energy could not be embodied and expressed through any ordinary feminine clothing style, though. It would always be too soft, too contemporary. Since she had no connection to ways of using power related to dominance and control, non of the traditional power attributes would do either. Her pinpointed focus on the core of any issue, as well as her unrelenting aim to "cut the crap" needed something entirely different. What I eventually came up with was timeless garments like robes and kaftans. It is still a work in progress.

My Inner Observer constantly registers what parts of me are active or passive in regard to how I present myself and interact with the world, even though I am not consciously aware of it. Drawn into some kind of setting or activity where there is conflict, I can be reminded to consult this Observer. He knows which parts of myself are involved, which have been pushed aside and what specific quality needs to become more visible and active. Through this knowledge I can tweak my clothing style by looking at which colors, patterns and garment styles can strengthen these traits. This "road to wholeness" is a continual dance between self-awareness and self-expression.

Using Clothes as Tools

N ow that we have consulted our wardrobe to figure out which parts of us are most prominent or dormant, and learned more about the language of colors, shapes, patterns and clothing styles, we can begin to use our clothes as tools to bring in new characteristics, and to meet the new needs that unfold in our process of growth. Figuring out how to dress to include parts of us that have remained unexpressed can be pretty confusing for a while. But as we do something happens. When a new color or pattern is consciously integrated into our present style, it begins to communicate with subconscious levels. Emotional patterns that seemed set slowly start to shift. With a slightly new style the way we see ourselves also begins to change. Others start to respond to us differently.

We might start by using clothes to turn up the volume on traits that need to be strengthened. We wear colors, patterns and styles that promote inner balance. We invite them to help us integrate characteristics that might seem to clash with traits that are dominant. Since experimentation regarding styles and colors is important during this period, swapping clothes or buying them 2nd hand is a good idea.

For some it is invigorating to deviate from their usual style. Depending on how sensitive we are, and what trait it concerns, it can also be upsetting. We can probably all think of a style that would make us feel really awkward. So sometimes it makes sense to tread carefully, while checking in on how we feel on a regular basis. Treading too fast or too boldly might backfire and bring up defense mechanisms.

Something to remember is that clothes are not just a language to tell others about who we are. Since we dress just as much for our own sake, the garments we wear are just as important when there's no one else around. It can actually be helpful to try out new colors or styles when we are alone.

As we begin to tread this path an ongoing process is ignited. Being authentic becomes a priority. Our desire to fit in, or seek attention, will gradually diminish. As we begin to discover our true Self behind our persona, and become more grounded in our core qualities, we can start to develop a clothing style that is more genuine, one that doesn't become outdated. From this point on we won't need as many clothes. The ones we have were chosen with care. If they are of high quality they will look good, and serve their purpose, for many years to come.

It is important to distinguish between the different tools available, and how to use them, when we embark on this journey.

Colors are an expression of our energy - the electromagnetic quality of our thoughts, feelings and moods. Figure out which hues in the spectrum you are less acquainted with and experiment by wearing them in a brightness and saturation that agrees with you.

Shapes represent different processes and psychological functions that are closely related to our personality traits. Which of the four basic shapes do you feel more or less comfortable with? Can you introduce those you are unused to into your wardrobe in ways that feel ok?

Fabric patterns are a reflection of different life patterns, which are a mix of feelings, states of mind and inner processes. As you explore your own life patterns it becomes more clear which type of fabrics you need to introduce into your wardrobe to become more integrated.

A clothing style is created through combining these three with garments into a complex whole. Try to look at your own overall style with objective, discerning eyes. Can you raise the volume of some facet, or tweak the expression of another? Use colors, shapes, patterns, fabric qualities and garments in a way that shifts the overall experience of what you are expressing.

Personal growth and self development has its ups and downs. It can also be confusing. Our inner journey can stimulate some serious introspection which, in turn, can shift our focus to negative emotions and thought patterns. It can get heavy. Adding clothes to the mix helps us include creativity, joy and beauty in this process. They also add a crucial sense of embodiment and bring our whole selves into our path of development.

We are each like complex universes. Since the uniqueness of each individual is a mystery to discover and reveal, there is no general formula to follow. Luckily there are some reoccurring themes in the process. Designing our identity is always a matter of balancing and integrating various characteristics that have become over- or under-valued, forgotten or totally denied. As this invisible structure of inner polarities looses its grip on us we begin to embrace wholeness, and can open up to higher levels of clarity and harmony.

With growing awareness that each of us is a field of conscious, dynamic awareness, it becomes obvious that the clothes we wear are an extension of this energy field. They are an integral part of any imbalance or lack of synergy in this complex system. Using our everyday garments to tweak and shape this field is as deeply meaningful as it is fun and rewarding.

Energy Medicine is based on the understanding that our bodies aren't just physical matter and chemical molecules. Vital energy flows through the human body and our biofield is affected by a variety of things. Our physical bodies and life experiences are informed by the energies in this field, and any imbalances or blocks can contribute to emotional challenges, physical pain or illness. Health can thus be restored by rebalancing our energy field.

This form of complementary and alternative medicine includes any practice or treatment method that stimulates the ability of the human organism to heal in natural ways. Many of these are thousands of years old. Acupuncture, homeopathy, reflexology, shiatsu and reiki are common forms of energy treatment, while meditation, yoga, and peaceful martial arts, or moving meditations, like Aikido, Tai Chi and Qigong are the most well known practices. Energy Medicine is thus a general term for different ways to enhance the flow of our energy to heal, to become more whole. Following this line of thoughts, it becomes obvious that the clothes we wear can also function as a form of Energy Medicine.

It is now time to create your own recipe! Remember that the conditioned personality is really just a pattern of functioning that has become set and thus more or less devoid of life. So interrupt the pattern! Bring in some movement! Wear a strict outfit to that meeting, dress up in wild colors at night. Mix or switch them around in playful and spontaneous ways. Let peace and modesty be your outfit on the day that follows. Wear red socks. Wear different socks. Wrap that beautiful neck of yours in scarves with crazy patterns. Allow your sensitivity to shine through flowing and transparent fabrics. Mend the hole in that sweater you've loved for decades with embroidery that brings hints about your journey. Wear clothes that show your sensuality.

Every change starts with an intention. If we hold on to that intention, and regularly act on it, it turns into a habit. Eventually it becomes our second nature. The most important thing is to follow our own inspiring path of growth and dictate your own clothing rules as we move along!

PART IV

Towards a New Story

You never change things by fighting the existing reality.
To change something, build a new model
that makes the existing model obsolete.
Buckminster Fuller

We have taken a serious look at the clothing industry as well as the prevailing system of beliefs in Western culture. We moved on to raise some questions about who we are and where we came from. Tracing our development during the millennia after the last ice age, we explored how the rise of civilization changed our consciousness, and influenced what ideals and belief system we ended up with. To gain a deeper understanding of who we are we looked at some identity models and then focused on the different needs clothes can fill in various stages of human growth. Finally we zoomed in on the art of designing identity with colors, shapes, patterns and clothing styles as our tools.

We have looked at what is and what was. It is now time to shift our focus to the New Story. As we do, a few questions seem vital: How can we change the course of our culture towards a sustainable and holistic narrative? How do we build systems that are in tune with nature and human growth? And since we focus on the world of clothes: How can we create an industry where garments are designed to be truly beneficial to the people who wear them, and where the well-being of textile workers, as well as our environment, is built into our ways to manufacture them?

A New Paradigm

The recognition of our oneness with all of nature was at the heart of the Old European and the Cretan worship of the Goddess. New scientific theories, like *The Gaia Hypothesis*, also claim that all life on earth is part of a single, indivisible and conscious self-regulating system, acting to preserve the conditions which make life possible. All living matter of earth, the atmosphere, oceans and soil, as well as all animals and humans, form one complex and interconnected living system. There is not even a particle that is self-sufficient. We are all dependent on everything and everyone else.

> Humankind has not woven the web of life.
> We are but one thread within it.
> Whatever we do to the web we do to ourselves.
> All things are bound together. All things connect.
> *Chief Seattle*

Many wise women and men, along with ancient prophecies, claim that we are living through the greatest transformation in the history of mankind, that will forever change us as a species. One of the truest signs of evolving human consciousness is our ability to hold polarities and to embrace complexity. This means letting go of the illusion that we are in control, that we have all the answers. It means being willing to think and behave in new ways, to acknowledge that in a complex world a multitude of perspectives are included. Embracing complexity also means to trust this larger organism – whatever we choose to call it – and have faith in its formative forcefield.

This leap in consciousness helps us make meaning of the emerging reality beyond that of the earth-bound larvae. As the butterfly leaves the chrysalis, and tries out its new wings, it enters this all-inclusive and inter-dimensional space. Without an ability to adapt to this new reality it would be totally disoriented and lost.

We are that butterfly. Even though this new and mind-boggling perspective might make us dizzy at first, we simply need to get used to it. This richer awareness unites the physical and metaphysical, the ideal and the existential, the personal and universal into one single narrative. It provides a new way of understanding ourselves and the world we are a part of. It creates the synthesis we lacked in our state of fragmentation.

Visionary Art & Design

Art can be visionary and "New Stories" are often first expressed through fiction in books and movies. Many who saw Matrix, Avatar or Arrival probably felt that they, to some extent, actually described our own reality.

In The Matrix humanity is enslaved and trapped inside a simulated reality. It asks the question: "What is real?" and focuses on finding a way out to a larger reality where physical laws can be bended and anything is possible. Neo, the protagonist, is given the choice between a red and a blue pill, which is really a choice between the willingness to learn a potentially unsettling and life-changing truth, or remaining in ignorance.

> You take the blue pill, the story ends,
> you wake up in your bed and believe whatever you want to believe.
> You take the red pill, you stay in wonderland,
> and I show you how deep the rabbit hole goes.
> *Morpheus in The Matrix*

There are no trees left on Earth and greed-driven humans are mining for the rare and costly Unobtanium on the planet Pandora in the Avatar plot. This planet is the home of the Na'vi, a highly developed humanoid race who live in harmony with nature and worship a Mother Goddess. The movie highlights the human lack of awareness as well as violent and destructive ways of interacting with nature and each other. It also paints a beautiful vision of a different way of life.

Arrival tells the story of a group of aliens who visit Earth. Even though they have come to help humanity, most countries assume that they are hostile and prepare to fight or kill them. The unique language of these Heptapods (note the connection to the heptagram) is non-linear and based on a circle. It conveys meaning, but doesn't represent sound or spoken words. If you learn it your brain is rewired and you begin to perceive life the way they do – holistically and beyond time. This universal language is the Heptapods' gift to humanity, to help us find unity and leave separation, hostility and war behind.

One of the reasons for the success of these movies is most probably that the connection to our time, our way of life and the challenges we are facing, is so obvious. We *are* held back in a belief system that limits our perception of reality, while most remain oblivious of it. And it *is* possible to question, see through and leave this "simulated" reality. It is also true that we are greedily depleting natural resources in a state of unawareness and disconnection from each other as well as our environment. To live in harmony with nature is not only possible, it is key to our survival as a species. And if our language was holistic and symbolic, and was based on a deeper meaning instead of sounds, it would lead to very different ways of perceiving things, with no need for aggressive conflicts.

> We are being given the opportunity to stitch a new garment.
> One that fits all humanity, and Nature.
> *Brené Brown*

So can clothes be visionary? Can they tell a New Story? One way of telling it is through a new, inclusive perspective where no color, shape, pattern or clothing style is idealized, since they are merely different expressions of the whole. As more and more of us embark on a path of exploring and designing identity, and search for ways to express our true

Selves through the ways we dress, it will be futile to keep looking at how others express themselves through the clothes they wear. This means that fashion – a system built upon an Old Story mindset, along with ways of behavior, idealization and conformity – will no longer be relevant.

We already know that the emerging stages of human evolution activate new needs and new sets of motivation. Our new clothes must be optimized to meet those needs. At this point of transition our job is to figure out how this is done. So let's use what we have learned to find ways to build a new foundation for designing, producing as well as using clothes, in ways that embrace our stunning human complexity and help us embody the New Story. As we do the Old and Worn-Out Story will fade away. Soon it will just be a memory of how things used to be done. Let's just take a brief look at how we can relate to beauty when ideals have become something obsolete before we do.

Taking Beauty Seriously

Superficial is a word that is often used in connection to clothes. Since this word carries a negative connotation, it seems to suggest that clothes (except for their basic and practical functions) are some superfluous decoration on the surface that is totally unnecessary. As if beauty and body decoration lack depth.

Maybe the true meaning of beauty has been lost along with the Worn-Out Story? Beauty is one of the things that is often left out for cost efficiency. How can a garment be valued if its style rapidly gets out of fashion? Can we talk about beauty if the fabric of a garment has been chosen for its low price? Is value a word we can use if the clothes we wear have been manufactured at the highest possible speed by stressed textile workers?

Creating beauty in our lives is an important part of human cultures all over the world. Among traditional as well as indigenous peoples decoration is still a part of everyday life. Even if you're in the tropics and it's too hot for clothes, you will see the most intricate string of beads or a beautifully woven loincloth.

The Omo people of Ethiopia paint and decorate their bodies with pigments from their environment as well as fruits, flowers, leaves or twigs. Mothers paint babies, children and adults paint themselves and each other, in a tradition that has probably been the same for thousands of years. The daily paintings are expressions of pure joy, and seem even more essential to them than music or dance. Their ephemeral art demonstrates that expressing ourselves through the decoration or our bodies is an important human need.

Everyone who has created a garment through crafts such as dyeing, weaving, sewing or knitting, and maybe even decorated it with needlepoint, printing or painting, knows that the value of these practices are so much more than the end result. Focusing our attention on making things with our hands is like a meditation, where we might occasionally find ourselves in a state of timelessness.

Behind these practices there is also a desire to express something that can evoke feelings of joy and beauty, in ourselves as well as others – the satisfaction in seeing, touching and appreciating what was first a vague idea. All of these feelings seem to permeate a garment that is made by hand with care. It is something palpable that can be felt.

So what is the deeper purpose to beauty? Some years ago I became intrigued by the word *adornment* (to enhance the appearance of someone or something) and the resemblance between *adorn* and *adore*. Was this just a coincidence? As I searched for clues I discovered that the word adore comes from the Latin verb *ad-orare*, which means 'to speak, pray or worship'. The deeper meaning of this word is thus not a feeling but an expression. I also found that an obsolete form of adore is adorn! So the original meaning of adornment was a way to express love and worship. To decorate ourselves would thus be a way to express deep love and appreciation.

> Everything has beauty
> but not everyone sees it.
> *Confucius*

At the heart of the New Story there is love and reverence for nature, for humans and animals. It goes without saying that this includes loving our Selves. Due to conditioning this might not always be easy. Many of us have been taught that loving ourselves makes us selfish and egotistical. But to love our Selves does not mean we are worth more than anybody else. If anything it makes us more capable of loving others. The art of adornment helps us practice this kind of Self love.

And the New Story Begins

Rob Hopkins takes us on a tour to people and communities around the world, who are in the process of creating a more sustainable society, in his inspiring book *From What Is to What If*. To further explore these ideas he invites people to his podcast and asks them to imagine what life would be like some years ahead if their project has been integrated in society.

Let's play that game and start imagining! We find ourselves in 2035 and a shift has already taken place in the world of clothes. How does it look? In what ways has it changed how clothes are made, and how we relate to the garments we wear?

Along with the transformation of cultural patterns and narratives, and a new focus on inner development, the clothing industry has gone through significant changes. Some new concepts have been born. One of these is *Holistic Design*, which is a different approach to the design process. It rests upon the appreciation of every person's uniqueness, composed of inter-connected parts. This shift of perspective has changed the clothing industry to the core. Any concept that is built on conformity is a thing of the past. The well-being of the costumer is now central and there is a growing arena for clothes that can assist the individual on their journey towards inner balance and wholeness.

The curriculum in most of the design schools has adapted to these changes. Since clothes are so intricately connected to different needs in human growth, students now have courses in clothing psychology. There are also several courses about colors and shapes that help students reach a deeper level of understanding their influence, as well as how to use them, in their design practice.

In his book *The Awakening Earth*, Peter Russel wrote about the birth of a new discipline, *psycho-technology*. It combines our growing understanding of consciousness with the knowledge and techniques of mystics and spiritual teachers. This discipline is meant to improve the functioning of our psyche, to facilitate a transformation of consciousness.

Healing Patterns is one of these psycho-technologies. This new concept uses the knowledge of the connection between certain shapes, colors and psychological functions to create visual patterns for fabrics. These can be used to raise the volume of inner functions that are weak, or to balance and integrate inner polarities.

Design has evolved from being the product of individual taste and disposition, to include the ability to translate universal qualities and archetypal patterns to colors and shapes. It has developed into a human-centered design that nourishes the soul. The designer's role is thus fundamentally changed into that of a curious and humble explorer who, through reflection, reaches beyond the personal to discover and interpret the essence of things. A developed aesthetic sense is, of course, also required to find a visually appealing expression for these forces.

As our consciousness expands, and comes closer to a state of wholeness, another dimension of patterns is needed. Intricate patterns made to express the natural flow between different states, as well as fractal patterns that are based on non-linear transformations, take us to a whole new level. We find ourselves in a time that has acknowledged that science, spirituality and design are simply different ways of looking at, understanding and finding an expression for the mysteries of life and the evolution of consciousness.

In this transformed culture we have moved away from constant renewal to the reinstatement of timeless qualities and immaterial values. Our beauty ideals have also changed and the supply of clothes is no longer limited by fashion trends. Clothes are highly valued and not something we buy on a whim. Since they are used for a long time they have become an important investment. This is why we might need advice from someone with the knowledge and experience required to help us figure out what garments we need for inner balance, integration and the expression of our inner beauty.

This is where *Soul Styling* comes in. The role is not very different from that of the personal trainer at the gym who can create individual programs out of their expertise of how to optimize the physical body, or the nutritionist who can test our vitamin and mineral deficiencies, or the composition of our microbiome, to give advice about which nutrients to include in our meals. The Soul Stylist is also an expert in their field, with a deeper knowledge of the interconnection between the visual language of clothes and the human psyche. Different methods to explore a person's unique characteristics and potential for growth are used in the process.

The production of clothes has been reinvented. Since a growing number of companies are now primarily driven by offering something of real value rather that gaining profit, the focus of many manufacturers is the well-being of costumers, textile workers as well as the environment.

Our bodies come in all shapes and sizes. To celebrate this uniqueness, and honor our individual needs and choices, a more flexible clothing production has been developed. We are no longer asked to fit into standard sizes. New measuring tools have been developed that collect all the necessary body data and the garment pattern is adapted to fit those measurements. Digital printers create the exact amount of fabric needed – and sometimes even the various parts of a garment – to produce the desired clothes in the fabric pattern we want and need. There is even the possibility of shifting the colors of a garment's visual pattern with optic fibers. Due to these new manufacturing processes there is very little fabric waste, and when there is we have found creative ways to reuse these valued resources.

Clothing production is based in local units, connected through larger networks, so longer transportation is rarely needed. All of this makes production easily adaptable as well as highly sustainable. Through the perfect fit, optimum natural materials and a manufacturing process that is well thought through, the garments created are made to last.

So how do we relate to these garments? Our clothing habits have changed from unconscious needs and behaviors into a self-conscious practice. We are aware of the power of colors, shapes and patterns, and the different ways to use them. We also know that what is hanging in our closet, or is folded in our dresser drawers, is not simply clothes. It's a set of ideas about who we are. This realization has led us to face these ideas, to look at what is real and what isn't, and to release the ones that are no longer relevant.

Now, as we open that closet or drawers, those ideas have changed. Since we are more familiar with the strengths and weaknesses of our identity, and the blind spots that can easily throw us off balance, we now have a beautiful and unique toolbox of garments to choose from when we need help to find our way back to inner balance. Some days we might need to boost our ability to be focused and seek out the colors and patterns to help us with that. On another our softness is essential for relating, or we might need extra grounding for some purpose. And then there are those days when it's absolutely imperative that our very core and essence shines brightly in its unique beauty.

This is when clothes are transformed into visual poetry…

There were times in our past when *The Fabric of Life* was partly torn.
Many threads that used to connect us were ripped apart
and this rupture in the human weave seemed beyond repair.
It could easily have gone to waste.

But those rips and tears brought us to a halt.
They forced us to explore why it had been so roughly handled.
Did we not appreciate this amazing tapestry?
Was it not valued and worth mending?

We matured and grew wiser.
We realized that a torn weave can be mended.
Its broken threads reunited.
The edges torn apart stitched back together.

The process of repairing the fabric of our human tapestry
is, in fact, already well under way.
When it is done it will be much stronger.
It will be large enough to hold expansion.

And it will be beautiful beyond imagination!

List of References

Aronsson, Gun Maij **Holy, Healing Pictures**

Braden, Gregg **Deep Truth,** *Igniting the Memory of Our Origin, History, Destiny and Fate*

Eisler, Riane **The Chalice and the Blade**, *Our History – Our Future*

Gimbutas, Marija **The Goddesses and Gods of Old Europe**, *Myths and Cult Images*

Hopkins, Rob **From What Is to What If**, *Unleashing the Power of Imagination to Create the Future We Want*

Juniper, Andrew **Wabi Sabi**, *The Japanese Art of Impermanence*

Liljeroth, Gunnel
Liljeroth, Göran **Hel, the Hidden Goddess in Nordic Mythology**

Russel, Peter **The Awakening Earth**

Shinoda Bolen, Jean **Goddesses in Everywomen**
Gods in Everyman

Shlain, Leonard **The Alphabet Versus the Goddess**, The Conflict Between Word and Image

Sjöö, Monica
More, Barbara **The Great Cosmic Mother**, *Rediscovering the Religion of the Earth*

Woodman, Marion **Addiction to Perfection**, *The Still Unravished Bride*

Yanagi, Soetsu **The Unknown Craftsman**

About the author

ANNIKA THOMAS grew up in Stockholm, Sweden, and graduated from *Beckmans College of Design*. At the top of a career as head of design for a large clothing company, a decision to resign gained momentum. Annika went on a quest to explore how clothes could be developed to be truly beneficial – for  the wearer, the environment as well as for cultural development. This eventually lead to a new job description as a holistic designer. Annika has written several books about her work.

While continuing to be intrigued by human growth and the development of culture, Annika keeps experimenting with the design of garments and fabric patterns. She feels most at ease in her studio – sewing, creating patterns, knitting and weaving – while pondering life's big questions.

For more, visit metamorfos.se.